CPA REVIEW NOTES

2019 BEC

SURYA PADHI

This Book is dedicated to my loved wife and charming daughters

CONTENTS

BEC CPA EAXM

1. Blue Print

This PDF document from the AICPA details all of the AICPA blueprint changes, effective in January 2019.

Areas		
Area I	Corporate Governance	17–27%
Area II	Economic Concepts and Analysis	17–27%
Area III	Financial Management	11–21%
Area IV	Information Technology	15-25%
Area V	Operations Management	15-25%

2. BEC CPA Exam Format

The AICPA has completely computerized every section of the CPA Exam. Additionally, each section contains 5 testlets presenting different question types. BEC has 2 testlets of 62 total MCQs, 2 testlets of 4 total TBSs, and 1 testlet of 3 WCs.

Format of the CPA Exam BEC Section

Testlet	Question Type	Number of Questions
Testlet 1	MCQ	31
Testlet 2	MCQ	31
Total MCQs: 62 (50% of your score)		
Testlet 3	TBS	2
Testlet 4	TBS	2
Total TBSs: 4 (35% of your score		
Testlet 5	WCs	3
Total WCs: 3 (15% of your score)		

AREA I:

Corporate Governance
(1) Knowledge and use of internal control frameworks
(2) Knowledge and use of enterprise risk management frameworks
(3) Identifying key corporate governance provisions of regulatory frameworks and laws such as the Sarbanes-Oxley Act of 2002

1   Corporate Governance:

1.1   Board of Directors

(1)   No Individual Authority
(2)   Act as a group, if a quorum (majority of the group) – Duly Constituted
(3)   The primary role of directors is to safeguard company's assets and to maximize shareholder return.
(4)   Declaration of Distributions to Shareholders – Including Dividends & Shares.
(5)   Fiduciary Duties – Directors are fiduciaries of the corporation and must always act in the best interests of the corporation. Must act in good faith. Duty of Loyalty.
(6)   Right to Rely – A director can rely on information from officers, employees, accountants, legal counsel, or a committee of the board whom the director believes to be reliable and competent.
(7)   Liability for Unlawful Distributions – Liable for authorizing a distribution that would be in violation of the law.
(8)   Corporate Opportunity Doctrine
(9)   The indemnification – Company can pay for legal fees.
(10) Limitation on Director Liability – If Directors act in bad faith

1.2   Officers

(1)   Officers are individual agents of the corporation who manage day to day operation and may bind the corporation to contract made on its behalf.
(2)   Selection and Removal – By directors and may be removed by the directors with or without cause.
(3)   Authority
    a. Actual – Oral/Written Instruction
    b. Apparent – "Title" CEO/CFO
(4)   Fiduciary Duties and Indemnification
(5)   Also, May Serve as Directors – But according to good Corporate Governance the majority of the board should be independent.

1.3   Sarbanes-Oxley Act of 2002

(1) Title III – Corporate Responsibility
    a. Audit Committee & CEO/CFO Representations

   i. Public Audit Committees – Public companies are responsible for establishing an audit committee.

     1. Directly responsible for the appointment, compensation and oversight of the work of the public accounting firm employed by the public company (referred to as an issuer)

     2. The auditor reports directly to the audit committee

     3. The audit committee is responsible for directly resolving disputes between the auditor and management.

     4. Auditors are to be members of the issuer's board of directors, but are otherwise to be independent.

     5. Audit committees must establish procedures to accept reports of complaints regarding audit, accounting, or internal control issues.

     6. The member of the audit committee must be independent (they can hold membership on the board of director). They can't be paid as consultant and advisor.

   ii. Corporate Responsibility for Financial Reports

     1. CEO & the CFO must sign certain representations regarding annual and quarterly reports, including an assertion that states (Section 302):

       a. They have reviewed the report

       b. The report does not contain untrue statements or omit material information.

       c. The financial statements fairly present in all material respects the financial condition and results of operations of the issuer.

       d. By (CEO & CFO) signing the report they have assumed responsibility for internal controls

         i. Internal control has been designed to ensure that material information has been made available

         ii. Internal controls have been evaluated for effectiveness

         iii. The report includes conclusions as to the effectiveness of internal control based on their evaluation.

         iv. Disclosures are made about any significant deficiencies of internal controls as well as any fraud.

     2. Improper Influence on the Conduct of Audits – Illegal

     3. Forfeiture of Certain Bonuses and Profits- If there is any noncompliance by CEO & CFO they will have to pay for restatement

(2) Title IV – Enhanced Financial Disclosures

   a. Internal Controls & Audit Committee – The enhanced financial disclosures associated with the issuer reports include additional details regarding the financial statements, internal controls, and the operations of the audit committee.

   b. Disclosures in Periodic Report- Disclosures are intended to ensure that the application of GAAP reflects the economics of the transactions included in the report and that those transactions are transparent to the reader.

     4. All material correcting adjustments identified by the auditor.

     5. Financial statements should disclose all material off-balance sheet transactions. (Operating leases, lawsuits, relationships with other parties)

6. Confirmation of pro forma financial statements – No false statements, no omitted material information.
   - Conflict of Interest Provisions – Issuers are generally prohibited from making personal loans to director or officers.
   - Disclosure of Transaction Involving Management and Principal Stockholders
     1. Principal Stockholder = Ownership is greater than 10%
   - Management Assessment of Internal Controls – Section 404
     1. A statement that management is responsible for establishing and maintaining an adequate internal control structure.
     2. An assessment of the effectiveness of internal control.
   - Code of Ethics for Senior Officer – Establishes 'Tone at the Top'
   - Disclosure of Audit Committee Financial Expert
     1. At least one financial expert with combined education and experience
(3) Title VIII – Corporate and Criminal Fraud Accountability
   a. Criminal Penalties for Altering Documents
   b. Altering, destroying, concealing, falsifying documents can lead to fines and up to 20 years in prison.
   c. Auditors must retain all documents for up to 7 years' failure to do so may lead to fines and up to 10 years in prison.
   d. Statute of Limitations for Securities Fraud – 2 & 5 Rule
      - The statute of limitations for securities fraud is no later than the earlier of two years after the discovery of the facts constituting the violation or five years after the violation.
   e. Whistle Blower Protection
   f. Criminal Penalties for Securities Fraud – Fines & up to 25 years in prison
(4) Title IX – White-Collar Crime Penalty Enhancements
   a. Attempt and Conspiracy
      i. Fraud includes mail fraud, wire fraud, and violation of the Employee Retirement Income Security Act (ERISA) – punishment will be pre-determined by the United States Sentencing Commission.
   b. Failure of Corporate Officers to Certify Financial Reports
      ii. Any party that certifies the periodic financial

1.3.1 Audit Committee:

(1) [Title III – Corporate Responsibility] An "audit committee," as defined by the Sarbanes-Oxley Act of 2002, is a "committee established by and amongst the board of directors of an issuer for the purpose of overseeing the accounting and financial reporting processes of the issuer and audits of the financial statements of the issuer." The audit committee is simply a subdivision (or a smaller group) of individuals on the board.

Issuers (also known as publicly-traded companies or public companies) are required to have an audit committee made up of independent outside directors with at least one financial expert. A financial expert must have the education or experience to have an understanding of generally accepted accounting principles and financial statements. This person must have experience in the preparation or auditing of financial statements of comparable companies and the application of principles in connection with the accounting for estimates, accruals, and reserves. The law also states that the financial expert must have experience with internal accounting controls and an understanding of audit committee functions.

The audit committee's core responsibilities are as follows

    a. **Oversee the financial reporting process** -The audit committee reviews and discusses quarterly and annual financial reports, disclosures (including the Management Discussion and Analysis section (MD&A)), and management letters with management and the external auditor. The audit committee reviews the quality of the accounting principles and the reasonableness of significant judgments.

    b. **Monitor the system of internal control** - This committee oversees legal and ethical compliance programs and whistleblower hotlines. It monitors the effectiveness and efficiency of the internal control process, oversees the performance of the internal audit function (the internal auditors report directly to the audit committee), and discusses risk management policies and practices with management.

    c. **Ensure open communication with management, internal auditors, and external auditors** - The audit committee serves as the direct contact with the external auditor on issues such as accounting policies and principles; auditing standards require that the external auditor communicates with the audit committee on a variety of subjects. The audit committee must mediate and resolve disagreements between the external auditor and management.

    d. **Oversee the hiring and performance of external auditors** - Duties under this category include hiring the external auditor, approving the audit fee, and preapproving all audit and nonaudit services. Independent auditors cannot perform certain services for their audit clients; therefore, the audit committee must preapprove all services performed by the external auditor.

(2) The member of audit committee

    a. Can't receive compensation for either consulting or advisory nature / roles

    b. Must not be an affiliated person of the company (including subsidiary)

1.3.2   Internal Auditor

(1) Should follow institute of internal Auditors (IIA)'s professional and ethical standards
(2) Should provide assurance on risk management and internal control
(3) The chief IC officer should report directly to CEO
(4) Should independent and competent
(5) Should be report indirectly to AC

1.3.3   External Auditor

(1) Help user of the financial statement that the financial statements are accurate and not fraudulent
(2) Must attest management's assertion of effective internal control as required SOX
(3) Jobs act exempts "emerging growth companies" from certain reporting requirement for five years, including external reporting on internal control.

1.4   COSO – Internal Control

(1) Committee of Sponsoring Organizations (COSO)

(2) COSO Matrix

What is COSO?	1. Defines internal control as a process 2. Provides internal control framework and enterprise risk management				
Purpose of internal control framework	To assist organization to develop an assessment procedure for the effectiveness of internal control				
COSO framework to achieve Objectives =>	O - Operation		R - Reporting		C - Compliance
Components of COSO => Principles of Components	C - Control Environment EBOCA	R - Risk Assessment SAFR	I -Information and communication	M - Monitoring	E - Control Activities
1	E - Integrity and ethical values	S – Specify Objectives	Quality	Both ongoing and periodic	Risk reduction
2	B- Board of Directors independence	A - Assessment	Internal	Address deficiencies	Technology control
3	O – Organization structure	F - Fraud	External		Policies
4	C - Competence	R - Change management			
5	A - Accountability				

(3) COSO framework has 3 objectives
   a. Operating objective – meant for entities operational efficiency
   b. Reporting objective – related to entity's financial reporting reliability, timelessness and transparency
   c. Compliance objective - meant for entity's compliance to existing laws and regulation.

(4) The COSO internal control framework includes 5 components and 17 principles

	C - Control Environment	R - Risk Assessment	I -Information and communication	M - Monitoring	E - Control Activities
1	Integrity and ethical values	Objectives	Quality	Both ongoing and periodic	Risk reduction
2	Board of Directors	Assessment	Internal	Address deficiencies	Technology control

3	Management	Fraud	External		Policies
4	Competence	Change management			
5	Accountability				

(1) **C - Control Environment**- The control environment is sometimes referred to as the "tone at the top." The control environment is the framework upon which all other principles are built. It is not as specifically designed to ensure that internal controls continue to operate effectively as is monitoring.

(2) **R - Risk assessment** - The risk assessment component of the COSO framework includes principles associated with management's consideration of the risk of material misstatement, not the assurance that internal controls continue to operate effectively.

(3) **I - Information and communication** - The information and communication components of the COSO framework consider those systems that identify, capture, process, and distribute information supporting the accomplishment of financial reporting objectives, not the assurance that internal controls operate effectively.

(4) **M - Monitoring** - The monitoring component or function of the internal control framework is designed to ensure that internal controls continue to operate effectively. Monitoring of internal control effectiveness is done to provide an assessment of the performance of the system of internal control over time. Monitoring is designed to ensure that internal controls operate effectively.

(5) **E - Existence of Control activities**- The policies and procedures implemented to ensure actions are taken towards completing the company's objectives

(5) Limitation of COSO
  a. **Human judgement** – Human judgment can be faulty and subject to bias.
  b. **Not error free** – Since humans are involved, breakdowns and failures can occur
  c. **Management override** - management can override control
  d. **Collusion** – Control can overturn by management or other personnel through collusion
  e. **External events** – External events can circumvent the internal control

(6) Types of Control

	By Time	By Nature	By Functions
	Preventive	Feedback	General
	Detective	Feed-forward	Application
	Corrective		

  a. **Preventive** – Control that attempt to stop an error happening, Examples are access control, Segregation of duties.
  b. **Detective** – Control that detects the error after the occurrence of error. Examples are bank reconciliation, Inventory count.
  c. **Corrective** – Control that reverses the error. Example maintenance of backup files, Insurance etc.
  d. **Feedback** – Control that evaluates the process, if undesirable adjust the process.
  e. **Feed-forward** - Control that project the future result. Examples are inventory, ordering program.

f. **General** – Control that controls the environment

g. **Application** - Control that controls over a process that is data input, process and output.

1.5 COSO - Enterprise Risk Management (ERM)

(1) The ERM matrix

<table>
<tr><td>Defined by COSO as</td><td colspan="5">In September 2017, the Committee of Sponsoring Organizations of the Treadway Commission ("COSO") published its revised enterprise risk management ("ERM") framework which is now titled ERM – Integrating with Strategy and Performance.
The new definition of ERM is:
"Enterprise risk management is not a function or department. It is the culture, capabilities, and practices that organizations integrate with strategy-setting and apply when they carry out that strategy, with a purpose of managing risk in creating, preserving, and realizing value."

The original framework called ERM – Integrated Framework was introduced by COSO in 2004, and since then the framework has been recognized and widely adopted by organizations worldwide.</td></tr>
<tr><td>What is ERM?</td><td colspan="5">The objective of the COSO ERM model is to provide an all-encompassing framework for managing risk throughout all activities of an entity.</td></tr>
<tr><td>Objective of ERM</td><td colspan="5" align="center">SORC</td></tr>
<tr><td></td><td>S - Strategic goals</td><td>O - Operation</td><td>Reporting</td><td colspan="2">Compliance</td></tr>
<tr><td>Component of ERM (New)</td><td>G - Governance and culture</td><td>O - Strategy and Objective setting</td><td>P - Performance</td><td>R - Review and revision</td><td>O - Information, communication and reporting</td></tr>
<tr><td></td><td colspan="5" align="center">GO PRO</td></tr>
<tr><td>1</td><td>Exercise board risk oversight</td><td>Analyzes business context</td><td>Identifies risk</td><td>Assess substantial changes</td><td>Leverages information systems</td></tr>
<tr><td>2</td><td>Establishes operating procedures</td><td>Defines risk appetite</td><td>Assess severity of risk</td><td>Review risk and performance</td><td>Communicates risk information</td></tr>
<tr><td>3</td><td>Defines desired cultures</td><td>Evaluate alternative strategies</td><td>Implement risk responses</td><td>Pursues in improvements</td><td>Reports on risk</td></tr>
<tr><td>4</td><td>Demonstrates commitment to core values</td><td>Formulate business objectives</td><td>Develops portfolio view</td><td></td><td></td></tr>
<tr><td>5</td><td>Attracts, develops and retain capable individuals</td><td></td><td></td><td></td><td></td></tr>
</table>

(2) Risk Responses – classification of activities as per risk mitigation strategies

Risk Mitigation Strategies	Avoidance	Risk Reduction	Risk Sharing	Self-Insuring
	Disposal of a unit, product line or a segment	Diversification of product offering	Insurance against loss	Tolerating Accepting

(3) Risk Assessment Technique

Risk Assessment technique	Questionnaire / Survey	Workshop	Event Inventory	Process Flow Analysis
	Sending forms to fill	Meeting, gatherings	Listing of events	Flow chart

(4) Types of Enterprise risk
   a. Inherent risk is the risk to an entity in the absence of any management actions might take to alter either the risk's likelihood or impact.
   b. Residual risk is the risk that remains after management responds to the risk.
(5) Limitation of ERM
   a. The future is uncertain
   b. No absolute assurance because of (1) human failure, (2) system breakdown, (3) Collusion across ERM, (4) management override.
(6) Expected value is one of the effective tools to prioritize the risk

1.6 Control Self-Assessment (CSA)

(1) CSA is a process whereby **operational employees or lower-level managers provide their perceptions and impressions about the controls that affect them.** CSA is more effective than questionnaires because it gathers information from more people and can allow anonymity. Employees can gather in team meetings with a facilitator (and use groupware to hide which responses are theirs) or we can send out anonymous surveys. We can use the responses as audit evidence (under the inquiry audit procedure).

CSA works best in evaluating and monitoring "soft controls"—those controls that cannot be evaluated using documentation, confirmation, or recalculation. It is perfect for assessing the control environment (or internal environment, when assessing risks in Enterprise Risk Management).

1.7 Marketing

(1) **Transaction marketing** practices that emphasize a single sale with no further interaction necessarily required. Customers are attracted to low prices and will likely return based on price only.
(2) Interaction-based relationship marketing says that sales further relationships, thereby driving more sales.
(3) Database marketing uses data as the foundation for identifying target markets.

(4) Network marketing is a form of referral and relationship marketing.

1.8 Managing incentive compensation

(1) A public company must have a policy for executive performance
(2) Shareholders can vote certain executive compensation.
(3) Types of Compensation
    a. <u>Restricted stock option</u> programs may reward current performance but also emphasize future performance. The employee must typically stay through the option strike period and the option is only valuable if the stock price increases.
    b. <u>Fixed</u> (formula driven) plans may or may not emphasize future performance.
    c. <u>Company-Wide performance</u> based plans may or may not emphasize future performance.
    d. <u>Competitive commission plans</u> tend to emphasize current performance.

1.9 Responsibility Accounting

(1) Responsibility accounting is a performance measurement system that divides and decentralizes a company into responsibility centers (i.e., decision centers) and compiles revenue, cost, and profit data according to the ability of an individual to control (i.e., be responsible for) and act upon said information. It is based on the assumption that every cost can be attributed to one individual in the company. That individual becomes responsible for controlling that cost.

Annual and monthly budgets and accounting reports are then customized and prepared for each responsibility center. Responsibility accounting allows the company and each manager of a responsibility center to receive monthly feedback on the manager's performance over controllable costs.

(2) Performance
(1) Effective performance measures have a number of characteristics. They should relate to the goals of the organization, be objective and easily measured, be under the control of the employee, and understood by the employees. Employee control of the performance measured is a characteristic of an effective performance measure,
(2) Types of performance measurement
    a. Financial - Gross profit margin., Return on investment, Economic value-added.
    b. Nonfinancial - Percentage of defective products.
(3) **Benchmarking** would be used by a company in comparing its financial data to publish information to determine if optimal results had been achieved. Benchmarking is the process often used to identify standards that define or quantify critical success factors.
(4) Total productivity ratios
    a. Consider all inputs and prices of those inputs.
    b. Is calculated as the quantity of output produced in a given period divided by the cost of inputs in the same period, not the sales price of outputs.
(5) Partial productivity ratios
    a. Are concerned only with the quantity of a single input (e.g., direct material or direct labor) and do not consider the price of the input.
    b. Is calculated as the quantity of output produced divided by the quantity of the single input used, not the cost.

1.10 Miscellaneous

(6) **Business Judgment Rule** - If a director acts in good faith and in a manner the director believes is in the best interest of the corporation, and the director exercises the care that a reasonably prudent person would exercise in a similar position, the director is protected against liability for the decisions the director does that turn out poorly for the corporation. This is commonly known as the business judgment rule.

    a. A director has not protected under the business judgment rule if he knowingly causes the corporation to undertake actions that is not within the power of the corporation to take and not within the authority of management.

1.11 Questions and Answers

1.11.1 Question

Able Corporation owns numerous businesses along the coast of Florida. The company's management has identified business interruption events as a potential risk resulting from storm damages caused by hurricanes. The company elects to not only insure its properties, but to "buy down" standard deductibles with additional premium. Able's response to potential risks is known as:

a. Sharing.

b. Avoidance.

c. Reduction.

d. Acceptance

Explanation

Insuring against losses or entering into joint ventures to address the risk is known as risk sharing.

The answer is A.

1.11.2 Question

Barker Healthcare Corporation's management is developing their risk assessment as they review plans to expand their nursing home chain into various states in the southeast. The management team has consulted published industry sources to evaluate both population trends and affluence in the region as a means of evaluating both demand, the ability to pay and the risk that populations may either not seek health care or may not be able to afford it. Barker's listing of risks from industry sources is a technique for risk assessment known as a (n):

a. Questionnaire/Survey.

b. Facilitated workshop.

c. Event Inventory.

d. Process Flow Analysis.

Explanation

When management uses listings of potential events common to a specific industry as a means of identifying risks or opportunities, the method is known as event inventory.

The answer is C.

Choice "b" is incorrect. Gathering management together to discuss or even brainstorm ideas in a structured manner is a facilitated workshop. Common industry lists or inventories are not techniques associated with facilitated workshops.

Choice "a" is incorrect. Sending out questionnaires to affected parties requesting opinions on potential events is the questionnaire/survey approach. Common industry lists or inventories are not questionnaires or surveys.

Choice "d" is incorrect. A flow chart of activities used to identify potential risks is a process flow analysis. Common industry lists or inventories are not part of the process flow analysis.

1.11.3 Question

The principle that protects corporate directors from personal liability for acts performed in good faith on behalf of the corporation is known as:

a. The clean hands doctrine.

b. The full disclosure rule.

c. The responsible person doctrine.

d. The business judgment rule.

Explanation

If a director acts in good faith and in a manner the director believes is in the best interest of the corporation, and the director exercises the care that a reasonably prudent person would exercise in a similar position, the director is protected against liability for the decisions the director makes that team out poorly for the corporation. This is commonly known as the business judgment rule.

The answer is D

AREA II:

Economic Concepts and Analysis
(1) Knowledge of economic concepts and analysis that would demonstrate an understanding of the impact of business cycles on an entity's industry or business operation
(2) Determining market influences on the business environment, such as globalization
(3) Determining the business reasons for, and the underlying economic substance of, transactions and their accounting implications
(4) Understanding financial risks and the methods for mitigating the impact of these risks

2 Economic Concepts and Analysis

2.1 Demand

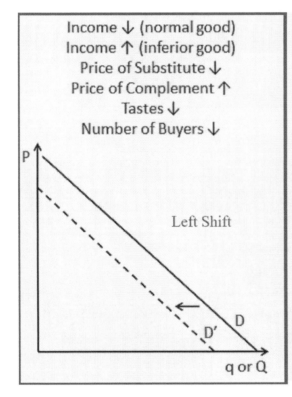

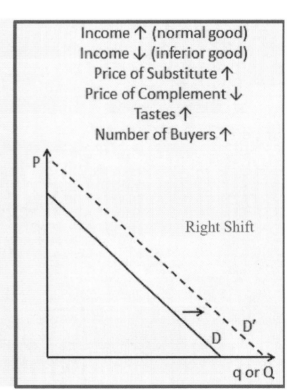

(1) Demand curves
    a. Represent impact of price on the quantity demanded
    b. Price is represented in the Y axis and demand is represented in X axis.
    c. Are negatively sloped
(2) Increase in income will cause
    a. ↑ in quantity demanded

   b. ↓ in quantity demanded for Inferior goods

   c. ↑ in quantity demanded of the complementary goods

(3) Elasticity

    1. Price elasticity of demand (Ed) = (% Change in QD) /(% change in Price $)

       ▪ Change in Demand = (Q2 – Q1) / Q1

       ▪ Change in price = (P2 – P1) / P1

Ed > 1	Elastic demand	Price ↑: Qd↓: TR ↓
Ed < 1	Inelastic demand	Price ↑: Qd Δ little: TR ↑
ED = 1	Unitary	
	QD – Quantity demanded, TR = Total revenue	

    2. Income elasticity of demand (EI) = (% change in QD) /(% change in Income)

Ed > 0	Normal good	Income ↑: Qd ↑
Ed < 1	Inferior good	Income ↑: Qd ↓

    3. Cross-elasticity of demand = (% Δ in QD of X) /(% Δ in $ of Y)

Ed > 0	Substitute	Pricey ↑: Qd X ↑
Ed < 1	Complement	Price X ↑: Qd Y ↓

2.2 Supply

(1) Supply curves

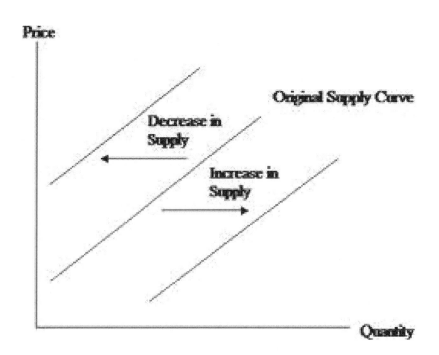

   a. Are positively sloped

   b. ↑ in price ↑ quantity supply

   c.

(2) Price elasticity of demand (Es) = (% Change in QS) /(% change in Price $)
- Change in Demand = (S2 – S1) / S1
- Change in price = (P2 – P1) / P1

(3) When the price of consumer demand (CD) increased from $20 to $22, the quantity of CDs demanded decreased from 100 to 87. What is the price elasticity of demand for CDs?
4. % Change in QD = (87 – 100) / 100 = 13/100 = -13%
5. % Change in price = (22 – 20) /20 = 2/20 = 10%
6. Ed = -13/10 = -1.3 (Elastic because > 1)

2.3   Marginal Propensity

(1) **Marginal propensity to consume / spend (MPC):** % of next $ of income that the consumer would be expected to spend = Δ in spending / Δ in income, MPS = 1-MPC
(2) **The marginal propensity to save (MPS):** % of next $ of income that the consumer would be expected to save = Δ in savings/ Δ in income

2.4   Factors influencing Demand / Supply Curve

Factors other than price in $ influence demand and supply of the product.

	Supply curve	Demand curve
Positive	(Increase in supply)	(Increase in demand)
	Number of producers	The price of the substitute goods.
	Government subsidies	Expectation of the price increases
	Price expectation	Consumer income and wealth
		Size of the market
Negative	(Decrease in supply)	(Decrease in demand)
	Change in production cost	The price of the complementary
	Prices of other goods	goods
		Consumer income and wealth
		Group boycott

2.5   Market Equilibrium (EQ) – Demand and Supply
(1) Point at which D and S curve crosses
(2) Represents the price at which all goods offered for sale will be sold
(3) Price ceiling (setting $ below EQ) set by government (Maximum price)
- Shortages occur as Qd > Qs
(4) Price floors (setting $ above EQ) set by government (Minimum price)
- Surpluses as Qd < Qs.

2.6 Production Costs

(1) A good should be produced + sold as long as MC of producing good < MR from the sale of that good.
(2) Over long periods of time, all costs are variable.
(3) Return to scale: ↑ in units produced that results from an ↑ In production costs.
- RTS = % ↑ in output/ % ↑ in input
(4) Economies of scale: as output ↑: Unit cost ↓
(5) Diseconomies of scale: as output ↑: Unit cost
    MC – marginal cost, MR= Marginal Revenue

2.7 Market Structure & Industry Analysis

	Most competition <= => Least Competition			
Types of Market=>	Perfect competition	Monopolistic Competition	Oligopoly	Monopoly
Number of buyer and sellers	Many	Many	Few	One
Types of product	Identical	Differentiated	Identical / Differentiated	Unique
Barriers to entry and exit	None	None	High	Impossible
Firm's influence over price	None	Moderate	Moderate to substantial	
Example Industry	Food Market	Shoes, clothes	Car manufacturer	Utility companies

(1) Perfect/Pure Competition – characteristics
- Large # of buyers/sellers
- No barriers to entry/exit
- Homogenized product
- Absence of non-price competition
- Ex. Mkt for commodities (i.e. Wheat, rice)
- The firm's demand curve is perfectly elastic (horizontal)
(2) Monopolistic competition - characteristics
- Consists of multiple suppliers
- Heterogeneous products
- Lots of non-price competition (advertising)
- Easy entry + exist to market
- The firm's demand curve is negatively sloping
- Ex. Retail industry
(3) Oligopoly – characteristics
- A few large sellers
- Heterogeneous or homogenous products

- Barriers to entry
- Non-price competition exists
- Rival actions are observed

(4) The firm's demand curve is kinked Pure monopoly – characteristics
- There is generally one producer
- No close substitutes are available
- There is blocked entry (patent) or government franchise (public utility)
- Firms demand curve is negatively sloping

2.8   Gross Domestic Product (GDP):

(1) GDP is the measurement tool of the output and performance of a nation's economy. It includes all final goods and services produced by resources within a country, regardless of what country owns the resources (emphasis is on the word "domestic").

    a.   GDP => Price of all good + services produced by a domestic economy for a year at current market prices.

(2) Real GDP = Price of all goods + services produced by a domestic economy for a year at an adjusted price level.
- Real GDP = (nominal GDP / price index) x 100

(3) Gross national product (GNP): Price of all good + services produced by the labor + property supplied by nation's residents.

(4) Net gross domestic products – Gross domestic product – capital consumption.

(5) Potential GDP - The maximum GDP that can be generated without a rise in the general price level.

(6) Two ways to calculate GDP (Gross Domestic Product)
- Expenditure approach
- Income Approach

(7) Expenditure approach to calculate GDP is GICE
- Government purchases of goods and services;
- Gross private domestic Investment (nonresidential fixed investment, residential fixed investment, and change in business inventories);
- Personal Consumption (durable and non-durable goods, and services);
- Net Exports (exports minus imports)

(8) The income approach to calculate GDP is IPIRATED
- I - Income of proprietors;
- P - Profits of corporations;
- I - Interest (net); Business Income
- R - Rental income;
- A - Adjustments for net foreign income and miscellaneous items;
- T - Taxes (indirect business taxes);
- E - Employee compensation (wages); -> Personal Income
- D - Depreciation (aka capital consumption allowance)

(9) Using the income approach, the relationship between GDP, NNP, NI, PI, and DI:

	GDP (Gross Domestic Product)
Less	Capital consumption allowance

NDP (Net domestic product (NDP) (at Mkt cost))

Less	Net foreign factor income
Less	Indirect business taxes
	NI (Net national income (NNI) (at factor cost))

Less	Social Security contribution
Less	Corporate income taxes
Less	Undistributed corporate profits
Add	Transfer payments
	PI (PERSONAL INCOME)
Less	Personal taxes
	DI (DISPOSABLE INCOME)

2.9 Business Cycle

(1) A business cycle is a pattern of **expansions** and **contractions** in economic activity. Economic activity can be measured with a variety of leading and lagging indicators, including gross domestic product (GDP), jobs, production, and sales. Understanding the phases of a business cycle can help to explain and predict the long-term trend of the economy, and the resulting impact upon a client's business. Auditors can identify and focus on areas where there is an increased risk of management override or circumvention of internal controls due to economic pressures on the business.

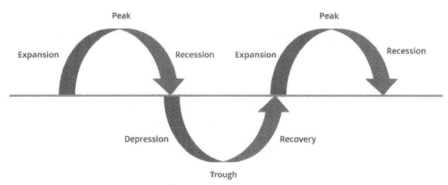

The business cycle is characterized by four phases and is measured as the period of time from the peak of one cycle through the four phases to the peak of the next cycle. The four phases of a business cycle are **expansion/recovery, peak, contraction/recession, and trough**.

- **Expansion / recovery:**

  In expansion/recovery, businesses are growing, new jobs are being created, wages are rising, and unemployment is decreasing. This can increase demand for products and services which exceed the supply, applying upward pressure on prices and driving inflation. In the extreme, overtime can become excessive and the utilization rate of plant and equipment can exceed normal levels. Firms may expand too rapidly, creating a risk that established internal controls no longer function effectively. Management may not notice or respond in a timely manner as they are overwhelmed by the production demands on the business itself. Periods of [higher] (aggregate spending

  a. Recovery: Period of expansion that follows the end of a contraction

- **Peak:**
The peak is the highest point of output during the cycle. The economy is operating above the long-term growth trend of real GDP. The economy is no longer growing, sales are declining, unemployment is rising, and economic output begins to fall.
- **Contraction / Recession:**
In contraction/recession, the economy begins to shrink. Employment level contract, consumer demand falls, and inventory levels build, depressing employee morale and price levels. It is often more difficult for management to meet their performance goals, increasing the risk that management may override or circumvent internal controls. Internal controls may be compromised as entities try to cut costs, resulting in unintentional errors or fraud. Disgruntled employees may find it easier to rationalize theft. Periods of [lower] (aggregate spending
    a. **Recession** -2 consecutive period of negative GDP growth. Potential National Income > Actual national income
    b. **Depression:** A deep + long-lasting recession
    c. **Panic:** A severe contraction of GDP occurring w/I a very short time frame
- **Through:**
The trough is the lowest point of output during the cycle, with high unemployment rates, a decline in annual income, and overproduction. This is the time at which the real GDP stops declining and starts expanding

- **Relationship between business cycle and economic indicators**

Economic Indicators	Boom (Peak)	Contraction	Recession	Expansion
GDP Growth	Peak	Slowing	Negative / Low	Growing
Unemployment	Lowest	Rising	Highest	Falling
Prices	Rising	Slowing	Falling	Low
Interest rates	Peak	High / Falling	Low	Low / Rising
Inventory	High	Falling	Low	Low / Rising

- **Leading Indicator:** Leading indicators change before the economy does and often provide some type of advance notice about what will happen. Stock market return is a good example of a leading indicator, as they usually begin to decline before the economy declines (and begin to rebound before the economy pulls out of a recession). Other leading indicators might be the average work week for manufacturing workers, changes in business inventory, new-home construction permits, and new orders for consumer goods.
    a. Ex. Stock market prices, average hours worked per week, new orders f/ durable goods
- **Coincident Indicator:** Coincident indicators move or change at the same time as the economy. Examples of coincident indicators are the gross domestic product (GDP), measures of inflation, nominal interest rates, government spending, and levels of import and export.
    a. Ex. Industrial production, manufacturing & trade sales

- **Lagging indicators:** Lagging indicators wait to change until a few quarters after the economy does. The monthly unemployment rate is a lagging indicator, as are the outstanding volume of commercial and industrial loans and the ratio of consumer credit outstanding to personal income.
  a. Example. Average prime rate for bank loans, Avg duration of unemployment, unemployment rate

2.10 Inflation

What is inflation?	Raise in price	
Types of inflation	Demand pull inflation - Higher prices caused by an increase in spending/demand. Cost push inflation - Higher prices caused by a decrease in Qs when production costs increase.	
Control Mechanism	Fiscal Policy	Monetary Policy
Who implement these policies	Government	Government + Central Bank
What are the policies they implement?	Increase consumer taxes Decrease government spending	Increase / Decrease in interest rate Increase / decrease in reserve ratio Selling / purchasing government securities.

(1) Common methods to measure price inflation
   (1) Consumer Price Index - The consumer price index (CPI) is an index used to measure real income by estimating the average price of consumer goods and services purchased by households
      a. Delta CPI = inflation rate = (CP1 (Current Year Price Index) - CP0 (Previous Year Price index)) /CP0 x 100.
      b. Producer price index (PPI) these measures the fixed basket of goods at wholesale cost to dealers.
(2) GDP deflator - This utilizes the total production of the economy as measured by GDP and is used to convert GDP to real GDP
(3) Recession - impacts
      (1) GDP decreases
      (2) Demand decreases
      (3) Unemployment increases
      (4) People don't borrow money
      (5) $ decreases

2.11   Fiscal and Monetary policy

Control Mechanism to influence inflation / deflation	Fiscal Policy	Monetary Policy
Who implement these policies	Government	Government + Central Bank
What are the policies they implement?	Decrease / Increase consumer taxes Increase / Decrease government spending Increase / decrease in subsidy	Decease / increase in reserve ratio Buying / selling government securities Decrease / increase in interest rate
Decrease / Increase consumer taxes	A decrease in consumer tax will increase disposable income of the consumers. This leads to a consumer will spend more. Increase in consumer tax, will play an opposite role	
Increase / Decrease government spending	Increase in government spending will increase disposable income of the consumers. This leads to a consumer will spend more. Decrease in government spending, will play an opposite role.	
Increase / decrease in subsidy	Increase in subsidy, will reduce the price of the product., thus increase demand. Decrease subsidy will play opposite role.	
Decease / increase in reserve ratio	Decrease in reserve ratio will increase the loanable amount, thus increase in investment. Increase reserve ratio will play opposite role.	
Buying / selling government securities	Buying government securities by government will increase money in hand of the consumer, thus increase in investment. Selling government securities will play opposite role.	
Decrease / increase in interest rate	Decrease in interest rate will increase the loanable amount, thus increase in investment. Increase interest rates will play opposite role.	

2.12   Unemployment

(1) Types of Employment
   a. **Frictional**: Refer to the time period in which people are unemployed due to changing jobs or newly entering the workforce.
   b. **Structural**: Represent potential workers whose job skills do not match the needs of the work force.
   c. **Cyclical**: represent unemployment caused by variations in the business cycle
   d. **Seasonal:** Result of seasonal change
   e. **Natural Rate of Unemployment** = Frictional + Structural + Seasonal (No Cyclical)
(2) Total Labor force = All individual above 16 and older either working or seeking to work
(3) Unemployment rate = (Number of unemployed / total labor force) X 100

2.13 International Trade

(1) The balance of payments (BOP) of a country is the record of all economic transactions between the residents of the country and the rest of the world in a particular period (over a quarter of a year or more commonly over a year).

(2) Balance of trade: Difference between goods imported and goods exported
  - Export > Import: Trade surplus
  - Export < import: Trade deficit

(3) Spot Rate: Exchange Rate for currencies that will be immediately delivered

(4) Forward Rate: Rate at which 2 parties agree they will exchange currencies at a specific future date

(5) Factors affecting Foreign ER
  - Inflation: Currency with higher inflation will fall in value relative to the other
  - Interest Rates: Currency in the nation with higher interest rates will rise in value.
  - Balance of payments: Currency of the country that is a net exporter will rise in value.
  - Government intervention
  - Political & economic stability

(6) Interest Rate
  - Real Interest Rate = Nominal interest rate – Inflation

(7) Bank Deposit Reserves
  a. Bank Deposit Reserve Ratio = Reserves / Total demand

(8) Federal reserve
  (1) Decreases bank deposit reserves / purchasing government securities, which in turn increases money supply
  (2) Increases bank deposit reserves / the sale of government securities, which in turn decreases money supply

(9) The balance of trade
  (1) Balance of payments = Exports (sale merchandise) -Imports (purchases) balance of trade + Capital accounts balance = balance of payments.

(10) Business Risk
  - Purchasing risk (purchasing power risk) is the risk that inflation will result in less purchasing power for a given sum of money. Assets that are expected to rise in value during a period of inflation have a lower risk. A U.S. Treasury bill is paid in nominal dollars, not adjusted for inflation, so the market interest rate for such investments includes an inflation premium.
  - Default risk is the risk that the borrower will be unable to make interest and/or principal payments as scheduled on the obligation. It is generally felt that U.S. Treasury bills have little chance of default.
  - Liquidity risk is the risk that an asset cannot be sold for market value on short notice. Treasury bills are highly liquid and do not require a premium for such risk.
  - Maturity risk is the risk the security will not be paid promptly at maturity. The risk of the U.S. Treasury not paying obligations is insignificant, so market interest rates on such securities do not include premiums for default risk, liquidity risk, or maturity risk.

(11) A cash flow hedge is a hedge of the exposure to variability in the cash flows of a specific asset or liability, or of a forecasted transaction, that is attributable to a particular risk. It is only possible to hedge the risks associated with a portion of an asset, liability, or forecasted transaction, as long as the effectiveness of the related hedge can be measured. [https://www.accountingtools.com/articles/2017/5/5/cash-flow-hedge]

(12)   A fair value hedge is a hedge of the exposure to changes in the fair value of an asset or liability. It is used to minimize fluctuations in earnings caused by changes in fair values.

(13)   Foreign currency hedging involves the purchase of hedging instruments to offset the risk posed by specific foreign exchange positions. Hedging is accomplished by purchasing an offsetting currency exposure. For example, if a company has a liability to deliver 1 million euros in six months, it can hedge this risk by entering into a contract to purchase 1 million euros on the same date, so that it can buy and sell in the same currency on the same date.

2.14   Globalization

(1) Moving towards more integrated and interdependent world economy
(2) Globalization of business divided into three categories
   a. Globalization of trade
   b. Globalization of production
   c. Globalization of capital market
(3) Drivers of globalization
   a. Global Financial Institution, example World bank, international monetary fund
   b. Reduction in restriction of trade and investment, example reduction in Trade barriers, reduction of investment barrier
   c. Technological Advances, Example advancement of information and communication processing, transportation
(4) Challenges of globalization
   a. Political system
   b. Economic system
   c. Legal system

2.15   Questions and Answers

2.15.1   Question

An increase (shift right) in aggregate demand causes:

a. An increase in the price level and a decrease in real GDP.
b. A decrease in the price level and an increase in real GDP.
c. An increase in the price level and an increase in real GDP.
d. A decrease in the price level and a decrease in real GDP.

Explanation

As shown below, an increase in aggregate demand causes the equilibrium price level to rise and equilibrium output (real GDP) to increase.

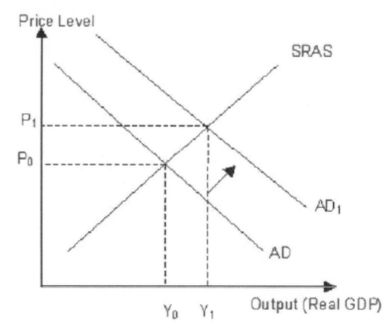

Choice "c" is correct.

2.15.2 **Question**

A period during which real GDP is rising and unemployment is falling is called a (n):

a. Recession.

b. Expansion.

c. Peak.

d. Trough.

Explanation

During an expansion, real GDP is rising and unemployment is falling.

Choice "b" is correct.

2.15.3 **Question**

Which one of the following most accurately describes the normal sequence of a business cycle?

a. Expansion, contraction, trough, and peak.

b. Trough, contraction, expansion, and peak.

c. Expansion, peak, contraction, and trough.

d. Peak, contraction, expansion, and trough.

Explanation

The sequence of a typical business cycle includes an expansionary phase, a peak of economic activity, a contractionary phase, and a trough of economic activity.

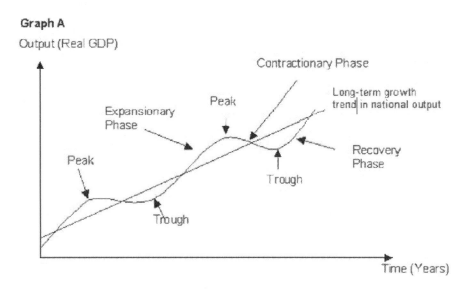

Choice "c" is correct.

2.15.4 Question

Tower Inc. sells a product that is a close substitute for a product offered by Westco. Historically, management of the Tower has observed a coefficient of cross-elasticity of 1.5 between the two products. If the management of Tower anticipates a 5% increase in price by Westco, how would this action by Westco's management be expected to affect the demand for the Tower's product?

    a.   A 5% increase.

    b.   A 5% decrease.

    c.   A 7.5% increase.

    d.   A 7.5% decrease.

Choice "C" is correct.

A coefficient of cross-elasticity of 1.5 would mean that a 5% increase in the price of the substitute would result in a 7.5% (5% × 1.5) increase in demand for the Tower's product.

2.15.5 Question

Given the following data, what is the marginal propensity to consume?

Level of Disposable Income	Level of Consumption
$40,000	$38,000
48,000	44,000

(This question is CMA adapted)

 a. 1.33
 b. 1.16
 c. 0.95
 d. 0.75

Choice "D" is correct.

The marginal propensity to consume is calculated by dividing the change in consumption by the change in disposable income. Therefore, the marginal propensity to consume would be 0.75 [($44,000 – $38,000) / ($48,000 – $40,000)].

2.15.6 Question

If an increase in government purchases of goods and services of $20 billion causes equilibrium GDP to rise by $80 billion, and if total taxes and investment are constant, the marginal propensity to consume out of disposable income is

(This question is CMA adapted)

 a) 0.75
 b) 0.25
 c) 1.25
 d) 4.00

Choice "A" is correct.

The **multiplier** refers to the fact that an increasemultiplierng has a multiplied effect on GDP. The effect of the multiplier can be estimated using the following formula:

$ Multiplier Effect = $ Initial Change in Spending × [1/(1– MPC)].

Substituting values gives: $80B = $20B × [1/(1– MPC)], therefore: [1/(1– MPC)] = 4. [Proof: $80B = $20B × 4]. If [1/(1 – MPC)] = 4, and (1 – MPC) = MPS, then (1/MPS) = 4, or MPS = 1/4 =.25, and MPC = (1.00 –.25) = MPC =. 75.

AREA III:

Financial Management
(1) Assessing the factors influencing a company's capital structure, such as risk, leverage, cost of capital, growth rate, profitability, asset structure and loan covenants
(2) Calculating metrics associated with the components of working capital, such as current ratio, quick ratio, cash conversion cycle, and turnover ratios
(3) Determining the impact of business decisions on working capital
(4) Understanding commonly used financial valuation and decision models and applying that knowledge to assess the assumptions, calculate the value of assets, and compare investment alternatives

3 Financial Management

3.1 Working Capital

(1) Need for working capital
    a. To meet entity's short-term financial requirement
(2) Determined based on benefit of current assets and obligation of current liabilities (Current Assets – Current Liabilities)

3.2 Cash Management

(3) Management's goal is to maximize float on cash disbursement & minimize float on cash receipt.
(4) The need of the cash arises due to
    a. Operational balances - Operational requirement
    b. Compensating requirement (minimum balance requirement by the bank)
    c. To avail trade discount – early cash payment attracts cash discount
    d. Speculation purpose – to avail speculative business opportunities
    e. Precautionary balances - To meet business contingencies.

3.3 Receivables Management

(1) Terms of Payment - 2/10, net 30
    a. 2% discount if paid within 10 days, otherwise full amount due within 30 days

(2) Account Receivable Turnover = Net Credit Sales ÷ Average account receivable
    a. Average account receivable = (Opening Balance + Closing Balance) ÷ 2

(3) Average Collection period (ACP) = 360 ÷ Account Receivable Turn Over
Or, Average receivable / net credit sales per day

(4) Cost of foregoing the trade discount or Annual Financing Cost (AFC)
   a. For Example, 1/10 net 30)
      AFC =

$$\frac{\text{Discount \%}}{100\ \% - \text{Discount \%}} \quad X \quad \frac{365}{\text{Pay period} - \text{Discount period}}$$

$$\frac{1}{=100-1} \quad X \quad \frac{365}{=30-10}$$

      = 0.1843%

(5) Benefits per check cleared
   • Benefits per check cleared = (D) (S) (I)
      ▪ D = days saved in the collection process
      ▪ S = average check size
      ▪ I = daily interest rate or opportunity cost (5% ÷ 360 =. 0139%)

(6) Cost of factoring

	The amount payable to factor [A] Annual Interest Plus Annual charge	
	Less – Saving [B]	
	Net Cost for factoring [C]	
	The annual cost of factoring (in %) = C / Amount received X 100%	

3.4   Inventory Management

(1) EOQ – How much to order?
   • EOQ = $\sqrt{\dfrac{2DO}{C}}$ or $\sqrt{\dfrac{2AP}{S}}$
      ▪ A, D= annual demand
      ▪ P, O=cost to place an order
      ▪ S, C=cost to store inventory

(2) Reorder Point: when to order?

	Average daily demand
X	Average lead time
=	When reorder
+	Safety stock
=	Reorder point

(3) Just In Time:
   • When to Implement JIT

- Order cost is low
- Lead time is low
- Storage cost is high
- Has a good relationship with suppliers.
- Impact of Just in
  - Stockout – Due to low levels of inventory, chances are there is stock out.
  - Carrying cost – Lower carrying cost due to low volume of inventory

(4) Inventory turnover = Cost of Goods Sold ÷ Average Inventory

(5) Inventory Collection Period = 360 ÷ Inventory Turnover
   Or, Average inventory / cost of sales per day

3.5 Sales Ratios

(1) Sales = Unit Price x Number of Units
(2) COGS = Unit Cost x Number of Units
(3) Gross Margin = (Unit Price – Unit Cost) x Number of Units
(4) Average collection period = Accounts receivable ÷ Average Daily Sales
(5) % A/R method to calculate doubtful debts. (Balance sheet approach)
- Calculate uncollectable estimate as % of end AR
- % based on historical AR w/o
- It may be accurate if you don't expect significant changes
- If you increase credit sales - it will change the relationship => not accurate
(6) % Sales method to calculate doubtful debts. (Income statement approach)
- Assume doubtful acct. will vary proportionally with variation in total credit sale.
- At the end of the month, multiply a % with total credit sales for month => Record this amount as doubtful allowance and bad debt acct.
- Strength: Matches bad debt expenses of the month with credit sales for the month.
- It may be difficult to determine %

3.6 Capital Budgeting

(1) Refers to budgets related to LT investment decisions
(2) Method of Evaluation of capital projects
- Payback Period
- Internal Rate of Return
- Accounting Rate of Return
- Net Present Value
(3) **Payback period:**
- Payback Period (In terms of Year) = Initial Investment ÷ Annual Cash Flow
- Disadvantages
  - Disregards profitability and time value of money
  - The payback method does not consider the life of equipment, salvage value, or depreciation
  - Ignores all cash flows after the end of the payback period.
(4) **IRR (Internal Rate of return)**

36

- Internal rate of return is the interest rate which will result in a net present value (PV) of zero.
  - PV of Cash Savings = PV of Investment Outlay
- IRR (PV factor) = Investment ÷ Annual cash Flow
- Accept project only if IRR > cost of capital
- Disadvantages
  - When evaluating mutually exclusive investments.

(5) ARR (Accounting Rate of return)
- ARR (ROI) = Accounting Income ÷ Average Investment
- Accounting Income = CF – Depreciation Expense
- Limitation of ROI
  - a) It could cause managers to postpone critical expenditures.
  - b) It could cause managers to not accept projects that would be advantageous to the firm.
  - c) It could be affected arbitrarily by allocation of indirect costs.

(6) Net Present Value:
- NPV = PV future CF - Initial Invest
- The present value of any single future payment is = Payment ÷ $(I + R)^n$
- Where r is the interest rate and n is the number of periods.
- Assumption
  - Discount rate / hurdle rate is known in advance.

(7) Cash Flow from a capital project = (Revenue – Expenses) x (1 - Tax Rate) + ([1]depreciation x tax rate),
  - (Depreciation x tax rate) is a cash flow because of savings in tax provided.

(6) Percentage changes for account balances for Year 1 to Year 2 = (Current Balance – Prior Balance) ÷ Prior Balance.

(7) Accounting rate of return
- Accounting rate of return = Net Cash Flow – Depreciation ÷ Average Interest.
- Ignores the time value of money

3.7   Profitability:
(1) Contribution Margin
- Contribution Margin = Sales – Variable Cost
- Contribution Margin Ratio = Contribution Margin ÷ Sales
- Break even point in units = Total Fixed Cost / Contribution margin per unit
- Break even point in $ = Breakeven Point (in Units) X Unit Price.
- Required Sales to achieve target profit = (Total Fixed Cost + Target Profit) / CM per Unit
- Margin of Safety = Total sales – Breakeven sales in $.
(2) Balance Score Card [FICH]

---

[1] Only tax depreciation is relevant. Book depreciation is not relevant despite its effect on net income.

- The balanced scorecard (generally a senior management or executive tool) is one such control mechanism.
- Gathers information on multiple dimensions of an organization's performance defined by critical success factors necessary to accomplish firm strategy.
- Critical success factors can be classified within various categories and are commonly displayed as: (1) Financial Performance; (2) Internal Business Processes; (3) Customer Satisfaction or Advancement of Innovation; (4) Human Resource Development.
- Financial Performance – Includes financial performance measurement, such as financial ratios.
- Internal Business Processes – Includes business process measures such as efficiency, quality of products and other key business processes.
- Customer satisfaction / Advancement of Innovation – includes measure organizational performance from customer viewpoints.
- Human Resources Development – includes performance measures like employee retention, technology development, cultures.

(3) The Profitability Index
- PI is good when comparing proposed projects with a limited capital available
- PI = PV of Cash Flow (Excluding Initial Investment) ÷ Initial Investment
- ROI (Return on Investment) = Net Income ÷ Investment
- Residual Income = Operating Income - (required rate of return X Invested capital)
- Required rate of return = Cost of capital
- Spread = ROI - Cost of capital

(4) FV measurement - based on availability of data for calculations
- Market approach- uses prices generated by similar assets sold in the market. Ex: real estate comparable prices for houses.
- Income approach – required PV calculation - uses valuation techniques to convert future CF to a single present amount discounted; measurement based on current market expect. About these future amounts.
- Cost approach - Economic substitution principle - based on the amount currently required to replace an asset (current replacement cost); value based on the cost to a buyer to acquire a similar asset

(5) Taxable Income versus after-tax cash inflow
- Depreciation is not a cash out, it just generates tax savings to arrive at after tax cash inflow.
- Taxable income = sales – operating expenses - deprecation
- After-tax income = Taxable Income x (1-tax rate)
- After tax cash inflow = Taxable Income – Tax + Depreciation.

(6) Degree of Financial Leverage
- Degree of Financial Leverage is the percentage change in earnings available to common stockholders related to a given percentage change in EBIT.
- DFL = % Change in Net Income / % Change in Net Operating Income

(7) Degree of operating leverage
- The degree of operating leverage (DOL) is a measure of the change in earnings available to common stockholders associated with a given change in sales volume.
- DOL = % Change in Net Operating Income / % Change in Sales

- DOL = Contribution Margin / (Contribution Margin - Fixed Costs)
    = Contribution Margin / Net Operating Income

(8) Other ratios
- Cash coverage = (EBIT + Depreciation) /Interest
- Gross margin ratio = Gross Margin ÷ Net Sales Revenue
- Gross margin = Sales – COGS (Cost of Goods Sold)
- Profit margin ratio = Net income ÷ Net Sales
- ROA (Return on Assets) = Net income ÷ Average Total Assets
- ROE (Return on Equity) = (Net Income – Preference Dividend) ÷ Average Common Equity.
- Price earnings ratio = Market Price of Stock ÷ EPS

3.8   Capital Management

(1) Before evaluating business decisions, we must determine the cost of capital
(2) Cost of capital = Cost of debt and equity composing the capital structure
(3) The interest of the rate of project > cost of capital => increase value of the firm
(4) Cost of debt: kdx = Interest rate on new debt X (1- Tax Rate)
(5) Preference Stock
   a.
(6) Cost of preference share = Amount of Dividend ÷ Net issuance price of the pref. Stock.
- kps = Dps / Nps
        10 / (100 — 5)=10 / 95= .10526
- Terms are defined as follows:
    Dps = Cash dividends on preferred stock (assumed to be $10 per share).
    Nps = Proceeds of preferred stock sale net of fees and costs (sometimes called "flotation costs") (assumed to be $100 and $5 per share, respectively).
(7) Cost of Common stock
   a. Discounted cash flow method = (Divided ÷ Price) + Growth %
- kre = (Di / Po) + g
        = (2.15 / 25.25) + .075
        = .0851 + .075
        = .1601
- Terms are defined as follows:
        kre   Cost of common equity.
        Di   Expected dividend (assumed to be $2.15).
        Po   Current stock price (assumed to be $25.25).
        g   Constant growth rate in dividends (assumed to be 7.5%).
   b. CAPM - Volatility of stock price relative to average stock
- Required rate of return for equity = Risk-free rate + Beta (LT average risk premium for the market - Risk-free rate).
- Beta = Measures correlation between a stock's price + price of the overall market.
   c. Dividend Growth Model
    - The Dividend Growth Model is a way to value stocks by valuing the dividend cash flow.
    - Value per Share = Annual Dividend Per Share ÷ (Required Rate of Return – Dividend Growth Rate)
   d. Gordon Growth Model

- $Ks = \dfrac{Dividend}{Price\,(1 - Flotation)} + Growth$

(8) Weighted Cost of Capital = Cost of Equity X % of equity in capital structure + Cost of Debt X % of debt in capital structure.

(9) Market capitalization is the value of a company as determined by the total value of its outstanding shares of stock in the market in which it is traded. It is calculated by multiplying the total number of outstanding shares by the current market share price.

3.9   Debt Management

(1) Types of Bonds
   a. Floating Bund - A bond with a floating rate will generally hold a steady market value because its value will not change due to changes in prevailing interest rates.
   b. ZERO coupon Bond - Increase in value each year as they approach maturity, providing the owner with the total payoff at maturity. These bonds don't pay interest.
   c. Serial bonds mature on varying dates, allowing an investor to choose a maturity date.

(2) Bond Interest
   a. Stated Rate
   b. Current yield = Stated Interest Rate / current selling price
   c. Yield to maturity

(3) EPS for debt financing = $\dfrac{(EBIT - Int\,for\,debt)\,x\,(1 - tax\,rate)}{\#\,shares}$

(4) EPS for equity financing = $\dfrac{EBIT\,x\,(1 - tax\,rate)}{\#\,shares}$

(5) Dividend yield = $\dfrac{(Dividend\,per\,common\,stock)}{(market\,price\,per\,common\,stock)}$

(6) Payout ratio = $\dfrac{(Common\,dividend)}{(Net\,Income - Prefrence\,Dividend)}$

(7) Economic value Added (EVA) = NOPAT - (Cost of Capital x Total Assets)

(8) NOPAT (Net Operating Profit After Tax) = Operating profit x (1 - tax rate)

3.10   Business Valuation:

(1) There are three methods (also called approaches or techniques) that the FASB recommends to determine fair value.
   a. The **market approach** to valuation, "uses prices and other relevant information generated by market transactions involving identical, or comparable assets or liabilities (including a business)" (FASB ASC 820-10-35-29). Find a similar asset that has sold and use that market value for your asset. An example of a common use of this method is in real estate: the average sales prices of comparable, recently sold homes are used to determine a fair market valuation of the home for sale.
   b. The **income approach** to valuation is an "approach that uses valuation techniques to convert future amounts (for example, cash flows or earnings) to a single present amount (discounted). The measurement is based on the value indicated by current market expectations about those future amounts" (FASB ASC 820-10-35-32). If the asset will bring in significant cash in the future, it will be worth more now. Likewise, if the asset return in the future will be risky, an investor would pay less for the asset now. This method requires

utilization of present value calculations and assumptions about future returns and economic conditions.

c. The **cost approach** is a technique "based on the amount that currently would be required to replace the service capacity of an asset (often referred to as current replacement cost)" (FASB ASC 820-10-35-34). The value is based on the cost to a buyer to acquire an asset of similar use; the value must be adjusted for deterioration and obsolescence. This method is similar to the economic substitution principle.

    i. The use of a cost (asset-based) approach for valuation is appropriate when:
1. The company is in liquidation.
2. The company is worth more in liquidation than as a going concern.
3. The company's value is basically related to the assets held.
4. The company has had no income in recent years.
5. Future benefit streams cannot be adequately predicted.

3.11 Questions and Answers

3.11.1 Question

On January 1, 2012, Colt Company issued 10-year bonds with a face amount of $1,000,000 and a stated interest rate of 8% payable annually on January 1. The bonds were priced to yield 10%. Present value factors are as follows:

	At 8%	At 10%
Present value of 1 for 10 periods	0.463	0.386
Present value of an ordinary annuity of 1 for 10 periods	6.710	6.145

The total issue price (rounded) of the bonds was

a) $1,000,000

b) $ 954,600

c) $ 922,800

d) $ 877,600

Choice "D" is correct.

The issue price of bonds is equal to the present value (PV) of the maturity value plus the PV of the interest annuity. The PV must be computed using the yield rate. The computation is

Amount	PV Factor	PV
$1,000,000	× .386	= $386,000
80,000	× 6.145	= 491,600
Total issue price		$877,600

The interest amount above ($80,000) is the principal ($1,000,000) times the stated rate (8%).

3.11.2 Question

For the next two years, a lease is estimated to have an operating net cash inflow of $7,500 per annum, before adjusting for $5,000 per annum tax basis lease amortization, and a 40% tax rate. The present value of an ordinary annuity of $1 per year at 10% for two years is 1.74. What is the lease's after-tax present value using a 10% discount factor?

    a) $ 2,610

    b) $ 4,350

    c) $ 9,570

    d) $11,310

Choice "D" is correct.

The net present value of a project equals

NPV = (PV future cash flows) – (Investment)

Since this problem involves a lease requiring only annual payments, there is no initial investment in this case. Lease amortization must be subtracted from cash inflows to determine income tax expense.

$7,500	Annual cash inflow
– 5,000	Tax basis lease amortization
$2,500	Taxable lease income
× 40%	
$ 1,000	Tax expense per year

However, lease amortization is **not** a cash outflow and is thus excluded from the calculation of NPV. The after-tax present value of the lease equals:

$7,500	Annual cash inflow
– 1,000	Cash outflow for taxes
$6,500	Annual net cash flow
× 1.74	PV factor for two years at 10%
$ 11,310	PV of cash flow = lease value

3.11.3 Question

Amicable Wireless, Inc. offers credit terms of 2/10, net 30 for its customers. Sixty percent of Amicable's customers take the 2% discount and pay on day 10. The remainder of Amicable's customers pay on day 30. How many days' sales are in Amicable's accounts receivable?

    a) 6

    b) 12

    c) 18

    d) 20

Choice "C" is correct.

60% of the company's customers pay in 10 days and 40% pay in 30 days. Therefore, the days' sales is equal to 18 days [(.60 × 10) + (.4 × 30)].

3.11.4 Question

Assume that management of Trayco has generated the following data about an investment project that has a five-year life:

Initial investment	$100,000
Additional investment in working capital	5,000
Cash flows before income taxes for years 1 through 5	30,000
Yearly depreciation for tax purposes	20,000
Terminal value of machine	0
Terminal value of additional working capital	5,000
Cost of capital	8%
Present value of $1 received after 5 years discounted at 8%	.681
Present value of an ordinary annuity of $1 for 5 years at 8%	3.993

Assume that Trayco's marginal tax rate is 30% and all cash flows come at the end of the year.

Calculate the net present value of the investment of the project.
  e) $105,000
  f) $ 3,585
  g) $ 11,216
  h) $ 6,216

Choice "D" is correct.

The net present value is equal to the present value of the future after tax cash flows minus the initial investment. The after tax annual cash flows are calculated by taking the before tax cash flows and deducting the income taxes. Since depreciation is deductible for tax purposes, income taxes for year two are $3,000 ([$30,000 cash flows – $20,000 depreciation] × 30%). Therefore, after tax cash flows are equal to $27,000 ($30,000 cash flows before taxes – $3,000 taxes). The present value of $27,000 received annually for 5 years discounted at 8% is $107,811 ($27,000 × 3.993). To properly evaluate the project, the investment in working capital must be considered a part of the initial investment, and its recovery at the end of year 5 must be discounted back to its present value. The present value of $5,000 received at the end of 5 years is $3,405 ($5,000 × .681). Therefore, the net present value of the investment is calculated as

Present value of annual cash flows	$ 107,811
Present value of recovery of investment in working capital	3,405
Less: Initial investment ($100,000 + 5,000)	($ 105,000)
Net present value of the investment	$ 6,216

3.11.5 Question

Spotech Co.'s budgeted sales and budgeted cost of sales for the coming year are $212,000,000 and $132,500,000, respectively. Short-term interest rates are expected to average 5%. If Spotech could increase inventory turnover from its current 8.0 times per year to 10.0 times per year, its expected cost savings in the current year would be

    a) $ 165,625
    b) $0
    c) $3,312,500
    d) $ 828,125

Choice "A" is correct.

If cost of sales is $132,500,000 and inventory turnover is 8 times per year, average inventory is $16,562,500 ($132,500,000 ÷ 8) If turnover increases to 10 times, average inventory would decrease to $13,250,000 ($132,500,000 ÷ 10). Average inventory would decrease by $3,312,500 ($16,562,500 – $13,250,000), which would save Spotech $165,625 ($3,312,500 × 5%) in interest.

3.11.6 Question

Kemple is a newly established janitorial firm, and the owner is deciding what type of checking account to open. Kemple is planning to keep a $500 minimum balance in the account for emergencies and plans to write roughly 80 checks per month. The bank charges $10 per month plus a $0.10 per check charge for a standard business checking account with no minimum balance. Kemple also has the option of a premium business checking account that requires a $2,500 minimum balance, but has no monthly fees or per check charges. If Kemple's cost of funds is 10%, which account should Kemple choose?

      a) Standard account, because the savings are $34 per year.
      b) Premium account, because the savings are $34 per year.
      c) Standard account, because the savings are $16 per year.
      d) Premium account, because the savings are $16 per year.

Choice "D" is correct.

The standard account will cost $10 per month plus $8 in check charges (80 × $0.10) = $18, or $216 per year. The premium account will have no fee, but will require an additional $2,000 ($2,500 − 500) of funds on deposit. The interest cost on $2,000 for the year is $200 ($2,000 × 10%). Therefore, the cost of the premium checking is less by $16.

AREA IV:

Information Technology

(1) Understanding the role of IT and systems, including the use of data in supporting business decisions

(2) Identifying IT-related risks associated with an entity's information systems and processes, such as processing integrity, protection of information and system availability, including those risks introduced by relationships with third parties

(3) Identifying application and IT general control activities, whether manual, IT-dependent or automated, that are responsive to IT-related risks, such as access and authorization controls, system implementation testing, and incident response plans.

4   Information Management

4.1   IT Governance

Mission of the entity	Provides practical steps to achieve entity's vision
IT	Then Information and technology should be aligned to achieve the entity's vision. 1. IT strategy support to achieve corporate level strategies, business level strategies and functional level strategies. 2. Due to supportive role and fast changing technology, it is important to have a well-defined IT governance and strategies.
COBIT	Represents as Control Objectives for Information and Related Technology) To implement the information and technology, COBIT framework aims three main components 1. Objectives: What is the business requirement that IT need to execute 2. Resources: What are the resources required to implement IT. 3. Processes: IT processes involved to implement IT

Domain of COBIT	The COBIT model has 4 main domains 1. Planning and Organization – Plan and organize IT system to achieve business objectives. 2. Acquisition and implementation –Deal the process and procedure to acquire IT solutions 3. Delivery and support – Deals with how IT system delivers IT services including operations, security and continuous service and training. 4. Monitoring: Deals with how IT processes with maintained for quality and control.
COBIT Business Objectives	As COBIT information technology system must meet seven very important business objectives (ICE RACE); Integrity, Confidentiality, Efficiency, Reliability, Availability, Compliance and Effectiveness. a. The system must be **available**. This means that employees are able to enter, update, process, and retrieve data as needed. Downtime should be minimized in order to ensure productivity. b. The system should assist the company complying with legal **requirements**. Knowing the information that the company is required to track and report, we can design the system to capture and communicate that information in a timely manner. c. **Confidentiality** of the system is a major concern. Strong passwords that limit individuals to only the information they need will help maintain the privacy of sensitive company information. d. We must be concerned that the system is **effective**. It should provide relevant, pertinent, and timely information in the form of easy to read and helpful reports. The system should supply the necessary information to make work easier, not more difficult. e. **Efficiency** is a business objective that a properly designed computer system can help us achieve. Information processed through the system should streamline the workflow and not create additional steps or procedures to make work more cumbersome. Information should be available when it is needed. f. A system with **integrity** accomplishes its objectives in an unimpaired manner. Processing is complete, accurate, timely, and free from unauthorized or inadvertent system manipulation. g. Finally, the system must be **reliable**. Reliability encompasses system availability, security, maintainability, and integrity. The

new system should be free from unauthorized physical and logical access, and any changes to the system should be made and communicated without affecting system availability, security, and integrity. We must design and implement preventive and detective controls to ensure and maintain reliability, and these controls should be examined regularly as the system changes and grows with the company.

4.2   Component of IT

(1) Component of Information technology includes:
   (1) Hardware
   (2) Software
   (3) Network
   (4) People
   (5) Data / Information

4.3   Hardware:

(1) **CPU**: principal hardware component that processes programs
(2) **Memory**: internal storage space
(3) **Offline storage**: devices used to store data/program externally, including floppy disks, DVD, etc.
(4) **File server**: a computer w/ a large internal memory used to store programs + data that can be accessed by all workstations in the network.
(5) **Router**: a specialized device that receives info. From 1 computer and send it toward its destination in the most efficient manner possible.
(6) **Gateway**: a computer that links 1 network to another.

4.4   Software

(1) Either system (Operating System) or application software
(2) System software: Comprise of operating system + utility programs
(3) Application software: Designed to perform specific tasks for the company
(4) Heuristic: Refers to software that can learn + to modify its operations (i.e. Spellchecking program)

4.5   System Design and Process improvement

(1) Consists of seven steps (A DITTO)

   (1) A – Analysis - During system analysis, the information needed to purchase or develop a new system is gathered.
   (2) D – Design - During the conceptual design, the company decides how to meet user needs. A physical design is then performed by the company, which includes developing detailed specifications used to code and test the computer programs.

48

(3) I – Implementation - All the elements and activities of the system come together during the implementation and conversion process.

(4) T – Training - Training programs are developed which include hardware/software skill training and orientations to new policies/procedures.

(5) T – Testing - System testing includes testing the effectiveness of user input, operating and control procedures, processing procedures, computer programs, and system reports (output).

(6) O - Operation and Maintenance - During its life, the system is periodically reviewed and modifications are made to solve any problems that occur or to improve the system.

4.6 Business Information System

(1) From the functional prospective information system included
   (1) Management Information System - Provides information to management, which may utilize it in decision-making
      ▪ Decision Support system => Assist in decision making. Combines models + data to help in problem solving with extensive user interpretation needed
      ▪ Executive Information system => A tool for higher management, sourced from multiple sources and a summary type of information.
   (2) Sales and marketing system
   (3) Accounting and finance system
   (4) Human resource system
   (5) Manufacturing and production system
(2) Expert system: Uses reasoning methods + data render advice + rec. In structured situations where human interpretation isn't required
(3) Types of reports
   (1) An ad hoc report is a report that does not currently exist, but that needs to be created on demand without having to get a software developer involved.
   (2) A demand report is a specific report that can be printed or viewed on demand.
   (3) An exception report is a report produced when a specific condition or "exception" occurs.
   (4) Scheduled reports are, the more traditional reports that display information in a predefined format and that are made available on a regular basis.

4.7 Database Management System

(1) The primary goal of DBMS is to minimize the repetition + redundancy in the DB, both to enhance efficiency + remove danger of information being stored in inconsistent places.
(2) It helps by
   (1) Providing department with appropriate information.
   (2) Safeguarding information from inappropriate access.

4.8 Data Processing

(1) Processing of transaction can take place either thru:
• With **batch processing,** the master file is updated only periodically, not after every transaction. At the end of each day (or at another interval) the operator may give the command for all changes made in a module (such as a subsidiary ledger or a payroll module) to be posted to the master file.

This type of processing is efficient and is used when all or most records need to be updated. For example, the credit card charges run through your credit card machine all day are sent to the processing company's master file at the end of the day in a batch. You receive a total of all of the credit card transactions that were sent, and this total posts in your bank account.

- **On-line batch processing** involves entering individual transactions into the file, but not updating or processing them until later when a batch is posted together. An example of on-line batch processing would be an Excel spreadsheet. If you open a saved spreadsheet, you can make many changes to it. The changes, however, do not become part of the master spreadsheet until you give the command to save it. At that point, all of the changes are processed (saved and made part of the document) in a batch.
- **Online, real-time (OLRT)** – Instantaneous processing of data. In OLRT processing, there is no time lag between information capturing and availability of information.
- **Electronic data interchange,** or EDI, is the use of computerized communication to exchange business data electronically in order to process transactions. EDI eliminates double entry of data, improves accuracy, and cut costs. EDI is more efficient than manual ordering.
- **End user Computing** – hands on use of computers by the end user.
  - Disadvantage of data being stored on laptop hard drives (no central DB).
    - Laptop stolen or damaged => data lost if no backup
    - Security of data at risk is no PW or biometric devices
    - Protection of customer privacy
    - No way of aggregating data
  - Mobile DB Adv:
    - Can be accessed from a laptop or smartphone
    - Mobile worker has access even when out of range
    - Needs consistent policies for data format, security and transmission.
    - Secure online storage is available at reasonable costs

(2) Data Structure
  - Size in increasing order:
    - Bit ▯ Byte ▯ Field ▯ Record ▯ Filed ▯ DB

(3) Order
    - Record ▯ Process ▯ Update ▯ Report

4.9 Data Transmission

(1) Network configures include:
  - LANs: Transmits info. Thru physical transmission media
  - WANs - use of phone lines, satellite transmission
  - VAN -link different company's computer files 2gether

(2) Different ways communication is org:
  - Bus
  - Star
  - Ring
  - Tree

(3) Special considerations related to EDI:
  - Strict stds req'd for the form of data
  - Translation software is needed

4.10 Programming language

(1) Source program: Language written by the programmer
(2) Object program: Language in a form the machine can understand (on-off, or 1-0)
(3) Compiler: A program that converts the source program into machine language.

4.11 Password Management

(1) The recommended characteristics of a password are
   a. Password length – longer is better, must be greater than 7 characters
   b. Password complexity – must contain a combination of upper case, lower case, special characters, numbers
   c. Password age – should be changed within a reasonable period of time (90 days)
   d. Password reuse – old password should not be used until a significant amount of time has passed.

4.12 Operations in an IT function

(1) Organization
   a. Data entry clerk: Converts data into computer readable form
   b. Computer operator: Runs programs on the computer
   c. Program + file librarians: responsible for the custody of computer programs, master files, txns files, & other records
(2) Control
   a. Control in IT operation includes (1) Logical control and (2) Physical control
      i. Logical control – Controls that are performed and control by software
      ii. Physical control – controls that are intended to safeguard the IT environment to provide continuous service.
   b. Data related control can be categorized as (1) Input control, (2) processing control and (3) output control
(3) Data control: responsible for reviewing + testing input procedures, monitoring processing, + reviewing + distributing outputs. Data control includes
   a. An **edit check** is an application input control that validates data before the data is successfully inputted
   b. Run Control - It is used to compare manual and computer-generated batch totals.
(4) General Controls
   (1) Relate to the overall integrity of the system
   (2) Involves segregation of the incompatible duties of authorization, recording, & custody (ARC)
   (3) Involves

1) Personnel Policies - Segregate authorization, recording, & custody functions
2) File security - Backup, lockout, read-only
3) Contingency planning – disaster recovery (hot Site /cold site)
4) Computer facilities – fire/insurance
5) Access controls

(5) Hardware controls:
   (1) Parity checks

(2) Echo check

(6) Application Controls
  (1) Designed to ensure that an individual computer application program performs properly
  (2) Application controls related to data input, data processing, and data output
  (3) Involves

	1) Input Control	- Check Digit ⬚ inputted correctly - Validity Check (valid SSN) - Edit Test ⬚ #'s in SS not letters - Limit Test - Financial total - Record count - Hash = a meaningless total - Nonfinancial total
	2) Processing	-System + software doc -Error-checking compiler -Test data -System testing
	3) Output - accurate	-Distribution list -Shredders -System testing

(7) Backup and recovery procedure
  (1) "Grandfather, father, son" system – A three-generation backup procedure: the "son" is the newest version of the file; the "father" is one generation back in time, the "grandfather" is two generations back in time.
  (2) Checkpoint and restart - A checkpoint is a point in data processing where processing accuracy is verified; if a problem occurs, returns to the previous checkpoint instead of returning to the beginning of the transaction process. This saves time and money
  (3) Rollback and recovery— generally used on online, real-time processing; A periodic "snapshots" are taken of the master file; when a problem is detected the recovery manager program, starts with the snapshot of the master file and reprocesses all transactions that have occurred since the snapshot was taken.
  (4) Remote backup service (online backup service) - An outsourcing service that provides users with an online system for backing up and storing computer files.
  (5) RAID—RAID (redundant array of independent disks). By placing data on multiple disks, I/O (input/output) operations can overlap in a balanced way, improving performance. Since the use of multiple disks lessens the likelihood of failures, storing data redundantly reduces the risk of system failure.
  (6) Storage Area Networks (SANs) —Replicate data from and to multiple networked sites; data stored on a SAN are immediately available without the need to recover it; this enables a more effective restoration but at a relatively high cost
  (7) Mirroring - Maintaining an exact copy of a data set to provide multiple sources of the same information

(8) A disaster recovery plan needs to include:
  (1) Recovery priorities,
  (2) Insurance,
  (3) Specific assignments for employees and departments,
  (4) Backup facilities,
  (5) Periodic testing of the recovery plan, and
  (6) Complete documentation of recovery plan (stored off-site).
(9) Types of backup facilities for disaster recovery plan

Cold site	Has all the electrical connections and other physical requirements for data processing, but does not have the actual equipment or files.	Least expensive. Generally takes one to two days to be operational
Warm site	Has all the electrical connections and other physical requirements for data processing, + actual equipment	Expensive than cold site. Generally takes one to two days to be operational
Hot site	Has all the electrical connections and other physical requirements for data processing, + actual equipment + files	Expensive than warm site. Generally takes few hours days to be operational
Mirrored site	Fully mirrored. Used for mission critical system.	Expensive than hot site.

4.13 E-Commerce

(1) Advantages
  a. No data entry
  b. Fewer phone orders
  c. Electronics online catalog
(2) Disadvantage
  a. Need to know accurate real-time picture of in.
  b. You can receive more orders than able to fulfill
  c. Add hardware and software for cc Pmt, security, backup large initial invests

4.14 Business process re-engineering (BPR)

(1) Does not start with what exists, but with future reasons for BPR:
(2) Reduce costs, increase profits, keep up with competition, senior management must be on board ambitious improve 100-150%

4.15 IT / Project Risk Management

(1) IT organization / project is subject to risk. These risks may be internal or external.
(2) Normally an organization follows a process, a risk assessment process, for example

a. Impact of IT on business, functions and survival of an entity.
b. Identification of information need
c. Categorization based on the impact of IT failure. This included prioritization of risks
    i. High impacted risk – Take immediate action to prevent and avoid such risk
    ii. Medium impacted risk – can wait for a few days, but needs to be fixed
    iii. Low impacted risk – can be ignored
(3) Risk response planning - options and actions to reduce threats to the project's objectives
(4) Future risk monitoring and control - may decide alternative response

4.16 BIG Data

(1) A new concept in data management
(2) Big data includes for Vs (1) volume of data is big, (2) Velocity of data of often, (3) variety of data and (4) veracity (integrity) of data must be derived.
(3) The data provides three types of analytics (1) descriptive – Description of data, what happened in the past, (2) predictive - provide information to take future decisions and (3) prescriptive – prescribe information to take certain action in a timely manner.

2019 CPA BEC REVIEW NOTES

AREA V: OPERATION MANAGEMENT

Operations Management

(1) Understanding business operations and use of quality control initiatives and performance measures to improve operations

(2) Applications of cost accounting concepts and use of variance analysis techniques

(3) Utilizing budgeting and forecasting techniques to monitor progress and enhance accountability

5   Operation Management

5.1   Product Cost Component

(1) The manufacturing cost of the product => Accumulated in Balance sheet. Called as inventoriable or traceable cost. These costs are represented as direct materials, direct labor, variable manufacturing overhead, work in progress, finished goods etc.

(2) Prime cost = DM + DL.

- The primary purpose of cost measurement is to allocate the costs of production of units produced
- High-Low Method – helps to segregate fixed and variable cost
  - Variable Cost per unit = $\dfrac{Total\ Cost\ @\ High - Total\ Cost\ @\ Low}{Total\ Unit\ @\ High - Total\ Unit\ @\ Low}$
  - Total variable cost = # of units X variable cost per unit
  - Fixed cost = Total Cost – Total variable cost

(3) Treatment of cost

Type of cost	Prime Cost	Conversion cost	Product Cost (COGM)	Period Cost	Variable Cost	Fixed cost
Direct material	X		X	-	X	
Direct Labor	X	X	X	-	X	
Direct manufacturing overhead		X	X	-	X	X
Selling and Admin overhead	-	-	-	X	X	X

(4) Flow of Cost in the manufacturing process

Direct Material	WIP	Finished Goods	Fixed Overhead
Beg. RM	Beg WIP	Beg FG	GOS
+ Purchases	+DM used	+CGM	+Under applied
= Available RM	+DL used	=FG avail	- (Over applied)
- (Ending RM)	+Applied MOH	- (End FG)	=CGS
=DM used	=WIP avail	=COGS	
	- (End WIP)		
	=CGM		

(5) Cost Volume-profit Analysis

- The contribution margin = Sales revenue - Variable costs (fixed costs are not considered).

- Contribution margin ratio = Contribution / sales

- Breakeven point – is a measurement tool, where the organization will have no profit or no loss.

- Breakeven in units = Fixed cost / (Price per unit – variable cost per unit)

- Breakeven in $ = Fixed cost / contribution margin ratio (or) Breakeven units X Price per unit

- Target Quantity to achieve target sales = (Fixed cost + target profit) / Contribution margin per unit.

- Profit margin on Sales = Income / Sale

- Margin of safety: Excess of sales over the BE volume of sales; measures the amount by which sales can drop before losses begin to incur.

- Margin of Safety = Sales – BE Sales

- MS % =   MS$ / Total sales

5.2 Absorption Costing

(1) is a GAAP basis accounting, where fixed overhead is allocated to cost of goods sold and ending inventory

(2) Both fixed and variable costs are assigned to units produced;
   a. fixed costs go to WIP and FG as inventory and then expensed as COGS when the unit is sold

(3) Budgeted OH rate based on machine Hrs = Budgeted OH in $ / Machine Hrs Budgeted.

(4) Budgeted Units to produce = Unit sales + Increase/decrease in inventory

(5) Budgeted RM to Purchase = Budgeted production X unit of RM required per unit of Fixed Cost – Increase / Decrease in inventory

(6) Under apply / over apply of overhead
   a. Under applied = Actual OH > Applied OH
   b. Over applied = Actual OH < Applied OH

(7) Treatment of under applied / over applied overhead
   a. Added to / deducted from cost of goods sold; or
   b. Charged / credited directly to income or;
   c. May be allocated to WIP and Finished good

5.3   Direct (Variable) Costing

(1) Include only variable manufacturing costs in inventory, fixed costs are charged to expense as a period cost when incurred

(2) The difference in income (or in profit) between variable cost and absorb cost:

   a. Income difference = Change in inventory x Fixed cost per unit.

(3) Under full absorption costing, a product cost is the sum of direct materials, direct labor, variable overhead, and fixed overhead.

(4) Under a variable costing, it is only direct materials, direct labor, and variable overhead.

(5) Overhead Rate = Estimated annual overhead ÷ Estimated annual direct labor

(6) The basic structure of a variable costing income statement:
   - Sales
   - Less: Variable cost of goods sold
   - Less: Variable operating expenses
   - Equals Contribution margin
   - Less: Fixed manufacturing costs
   - Less: Fixed selling and Adm. Costs
   - Equals: Net Operating Income

5.4   Variable vs Absorption Costing

(1) Behavior of cost

Absorption/Full Costing	Direct/Variable/CM
Product costs: includes BOTH variable + fixed manufacturing OH cost in COGS	Product costs: Includes only variable COGS
Fixed MOH is allocated to product cost based on units sold. Rest is absorbed into End Inventory (EI)	100% of Fixed MOH is expensed as "period cost"
Selling variable / Selling fixed cost always is a period cost.	Selling variable / Selling fixed cost always is a period cost.

(2) Behavior of profit when production ≠ sales

Absorption costing		Variable or Direct costing
Production	> Sales	Greater Absorption income
Production	< Sales	Greater Direct income
Production	= Sales	Greater Direct income

(3) Reconciliation between two method of income statement

		Absorption costing	Variable or Direct costing
Direct material		Same	Same
Direct labor		Same	Same
Variable manufacturing OH		Same	Same
Opening Inv X Fix.cost / Unit	XXX.XXX		
Less Closing Inv. X Fix.cost / Unit	XXX.XXX		
Difference	XXX.XXX		
Positive		XXX.XXX	
Negative			XXX.XXX

The only difference between two method is difference of opening and closing inventory treatment.

5.5 Activity Based Costing

(1) Activity-based costing divides the production process into activities where costs are accumulated. The production process assumes activities consume resources (direct materials, direct labor, and manufacturing overhead), and that the outcome of the production process requires the performance of the activities.

(2) Allocate costs based on activities/cost-drivers

(3) Enables manager to segregate cost into value-added or non-value-added costs

(4) This is not acceptable for external reporting and useful for internal reporting to management.

(5) Costs can be allocated in 2 ways:
- Direct allocation: Cost is allocated from each service department directly to product department
- Indirect Allocation- Cost is allocated from each service department to other service department(s) and production department, then to product department.

5.6   Process Costing

(1) Can be implemented where products are inexpensive and / or homogeneous, cost can't be identified to units / batches.

(2) Transfer to another department is always treated 100 % complete. Direct material of 2nd department is always equal to cost of 1st department.

(3) Average cost is used for transferring out to WIP and finished goods

(4) Equivalent unit is used to allocate cost

(5) Equivalent units produced can be calculated two ways FIFO and weighted average

    (1) FIFO and weighted average produce the same equivalent units when there is no beginning inventory. FIFO is a three-step process, while weighted average is a two-step process. The major difference between the two methods is consideration of beginning inventory amounts by FIFO.

    (2) Weighted unit Under FIFO

	Unit Completed during the period	XXX.XX
Add	Ending WIP X % completed	XXX.XX
Less	Beginning WIP X % Completed in last period	XXX.XX

    (3) Weighted units Under weighted average

Add	Unit Completed	XXX.XX
Add	Ending WIP X % completed	XXX.XX

(6) Unit cost of production

    (1) Weighted Average =

$$\text{Weighted Average} \quad \frac{\text{Beginning cost + Current cost}}{\text{Equivalent units}}$$

    (2) FIFO

$$\text{FIFO -} \quad \frac{\text{Current cost only}}{\text{Equivalent units}}$$

(7) Spoilage / Scrap

    (1) Normal Spoilage -> Considered for calculation of product cost

    (2) Abnormal spoilage -> A period cost, charged to income

    (3) Proceed from scrap -> can be treated either of the following ways

       ▪ Added to income, reduced from cost of sales

5.7   Joint Product Costing

(1) Applied when two or more product produced from manufacturing process
(2) Joint cost allocation basis
    (1) By physical quantity
    (2) By relative sales value
    (3) By net realizable value
(3) Relative sales value at split-off. - Defined as Sales price less the cost to complete. In other words, this is the additional contribution to income generated by completing the product.
(4) Sales Value at split-off
    (1) Allocate the joint cost of only primary products, not by-product
(5) By product
    (1) Represents minor incidental product generated out of manufacturing process
    (2) Revenue from sale of by-product can be used to reduce joint cost or treated as income.
(6) Process costing is used where the product is composed of mass-produced homogeneous units such as:
    (1) Gasoline and oil
    (2) Chemicals
    (3) Steel
    (4) Textiles (wallpaper)
    (5) And many more.

5.8 Job Costing

(1) Can be implemented where the product is expensive, heterogeneous products- cost based per job.
(2) Cost related to product is collected in a separate cost object and treated as cost of goods sold at the time of sales.
(3) Job costing is used in the production of tailor-made or unique goods, including:

    (1) Construction of buildings or ships
    (2) Aircraft assembly
    (3) Printing
    (4) Special-purpose machinery (microcomputer manufacturer)
    (5) Public accounting firm
    (6) Management consulting firm
    (7) Repair shops
    (8) Industrial research projects

5.9 Standard Costing

(1) Standard costs are usually associated with a manufacturing company's costs of direct material, direct labor, and manufacturing overhead.
(2) If actual costs are greater than standard costs the variance is unfavorable. An unfavorable variance tells management that if everything else stays constant the company's actual profit will be less than planned.
(3) If actual costs are less than standard costs the variance is favorable. A favorable variance tells management that if everything else stays constant the actual profit will likely exceed the planned profit.

(4) Material Variances

1	2	3	4
SRSQ	SRAQ	ARSQ	ARAQ

SR = Standard Rate, SQ = Standard Quantity, AR = Actual Rate, AQ = Actual Quantity

(1) Material quantity (usage) variance [1 - 2] = SRSQ - SRAQ

(2) Material mix variance = [2-3] = SRAQ - ARSQ

(3) Material Price variance [2 - 4] = SRAQ - ARAQ

(4) Total variance [1 – 4] = SRSQ - ARAQ = material usage variance + material price variance.
  If the result is negative, then the variance is un favorable

(5) Labor Variances

1	2	3	4
SRSH	SRAH	ARSH	ARAH

SR = Standard Rate, SH = Standard Hours, AR = Actual Rate, AH = Actual Hours

(1) DL Efficiency (usage) variance [1 - 2] = SRSH - SRAH

(2) DL rate Variance [2 - 4] = SRAH - ARAH

(3) DL mix variance [2 - 3] = SRAH - ARSH

(4) Total variance [1 – 4] = SRSH - ARAH = DL Efficiency (usage) variance + DL Price Variance
  If the result is negative, then the variance is un favorable

(6) Variable Overhead

1	2	3	4
SRSH	SRAH	ARSH	ARAH

SR = Standard Rate, SH = Standard Hours, AR = Actual Rate, AH = Actual Hours

(1) Overhead efficiency variance [1 - 2] = SRSH - SRAH

(2) Overhead rate Variance [2 - 4] = SRAH - ARAH

(3) Total variance [1 – 4] = SRSH - ARAH = OH Efficiency variance + OH rate Variance
  If the result is negative, then the variance is un favorable

(7) Flexible Budget Variance

  (1) Actual cost compared to Flexible budget cost

(8) Fixed Overhead Spend Variance

1	2	3	4
SRSH	SRBH	SRBH	ARAH

SR = Standard Rate, SH = Standard Hours, BH = Budgeted Hours, AR = Actual Rate, AH = Actual Hours

(1) Volume Variance = 1 – 2

(2) Efficiency variance = 2 – 3

(3) Spending variance = 3 – 4

5.10 Special Orders

(1) Special order represents, in frequent orders or customer specific orders. This type of order always need special attention in terms of cost, process and design.
(2) Whether the special order is undertaken or not depends on present capacity to produce such as (1) have capacity to produce (2) currently running in full capacity

	Have capacity to produce	Currently running in full capacity
Variable cost	Include the variable cost to produce the special order.	Include the variable cost to produce the special order.
Fixed Cost	Only include incremental cost	Only include incremental cost
Cost of sacrifice		Opportunity cost = Profit scarified for not producing the current product.

5.11 Planning

(1) A continuity plan explains how a business would recover its operations or move operations to another location after damage by events like natural disasters, theft, or flooding.
(2) Capacity planning is the process of determining production needs to meet changing demands for products.
(3) Budget planning is the process of creating a quantitative plan that estimates revenues, expenses, and capital spending for a period of time.
(4) Strategy (strategic) planning is the process of defining an entity's direction/strategy and making decisions to appropriately allocate resources to achieve this strategy.
(5) Sales forecast
  (1) Is the first step in forecasting projection of the volume and $ of sales for future is important because all numbers in financial forecast are based on sales forecast
    ▪ If too low => not enough capacity to meet demand
    ▪ Too high => excess capacity
  (2) Is considered by predicting economic condition, customer anticipated needs, industry trends, what products will be sold, new products?, Intl expansion? Exchange rates
(6) Strategic Planning: Setting of Long Term overall goals + policies
  SWOT (Strength, Weakness, Opportunities and Threats)
    ▪ It is a strategic planning
    ▪ helps clarify the factors favorable / unfav. for achieving Obj.
    ▪ **Strengths - Weaknesses = Internal factors**
      • Strengths - resources and capabilities to develop a competitive advantage.
      • Weaknesses - Gives competitors advantage over external factors:
    ▪ **Opportunities - Threats = External Factors**
      • Opportunities - Chances to maximize profits; we must look in environ in which we operate.
      • Threats - Dangers in the way of achieving goals - ex: new sales tax
(7) Tactical Planning: Focuses on Sort Term objective + temporary tech.
(8) Master Budget: Summarizes the results of all the firm's individual budgets (operating + financial) into a set of projected financial statement + schedules.

(9) Static Budget: Budget at a specific level of activity
- Can be for a division of a company or company as whole

(10) Flexible Budget – Budget based on various level of activities
- Advantage of flexible budget is that it can adapt to changes in VC that result from changes in sales levels

(11) Regression Analysis:

   (1) Linear regression is a method for studying the relationship between two or more variables. Using regression analysis, variation in the dependent variable is explained using one or more independent variables. The dependent variable is specified to be a linear function of the one or more independent variables.

   (2) Regression analysis seeks to identify change in a dependent variable (such as cost) related to change in an independent variable (such as a cost driver).

   (3) Degree of relation
      a. R=1-> Strong direct relation
      b. R=-1 ->Strong indirect relation
      c. R=0 -> No relation

   (4) Simple regression estimates a relationship between one dependent variable and one independent variable.

$$Y = a + b(X)$$

Total Cost = Fixed Cost + Variable rate X Units

   (5) Multiple regression estimates a relationship between one dependent variable and two or more independent variables. Thus, multiple regression has more independent variables than does simple regression.

5.12 Quality

(1) Cost of Quality

	Conformation Cost		Non-Confirmation Cost	
	Prevention cost	**Appraisal cost**	**Internal failure cost**	**External failure cost**
Purpose	The cost of any quality activity designed to help do the job right the first time. Examples of prevention cost include:	Involves any activity designed to appraise, test, or check for defective products. Examples of appraisal costs include:	The costs incurred when substandard products are produced but discovered before shipment to the customer. Examples of internal failure costs include:	The cost incurred for products that do not meet requirements of the customer and have reached the customer. Examples of external failure costs include:
Includes	Quality engineering Quality training Quality circles Statistical process	Testing and inspection of incoming materials Testing and inspection of in-	Scrap Spoilage Rework Rework labor and overhead	Cost of field servicing and handling complaints Warranty repairs

control activities Supervision of prevention activities Quality data gathering, analysis, and reporting Quality improvement projects Technical support provided to suppliers Audits of the effectiveness of the quality system	process goods Final product testing and inspection Supplies used in testing and inspection Supervision of testing and inspection activities Depreciation of test equipment Maintenance of test equipment Plant utilities in the inspection area Field testing and appraisal at customer site	Reinspection of reworked products Retesting of reworked products Downtime caused by quality problems Disposal of defective products Analysis of the cause of defects in production Reentering data because of keying errors Debugging software errors	and replacements Product recalls Liability arising from defective products Returns and allowances arising from quality problems Lost sales arising from reputation for poor quality

(2) 6 sigma - Total quality management - set of techniques and tools to process improvement.
    a. There are two major methodologies used within Six Sigma (1) DMAIC and (2) DMADV

Mnemonics	
DMAIC	D- Define Problem M – Measure Key Aspects of current problem A – Analyze data I – Improve / Optimize current processes C – Control
DMADV	D- Define Problem M – Measure Key Aspects of current problem A – Analyze data I – Improve / Optimize current processes C – Control

(1) **A Fishbone diagram** describes a process, the contributions to the process, and the potential problems that could occur at each phase of a process. The process is represented by a single horizontal line while the contributions to the process are represented by diagonal lines that create the image of a Fishbone. Fishbone diagrams provide a framework for managers to analyze the problems that contribute to the occurrence of defects.

(2) **A control chart** shows the performance of a process in relation to acceptable upper and lower limits of deviation. Performance 'Within the limits is termed statistical control.

Processes are designed to ensure that performance consistently falls 'Within the acceptable range of error.

(3) **A Pareto diagram** represents an individual and the cumulative graphical analysis of errors by type. Individual error types are represented on a histogram (bar graph), while the cumulative number of errors is presented in a line graph. The Pareto diagram is used to prioritize process improvement efforts.

(4) **A value chain analysis** is a macro level flowchart that shows the relationship between broad functional areas, the product delivered by the organization, and the way value is added at each link in the chain.

5.13 Ratios

(1) Asset turnover = Sales / Assets

(2) Return on assets = Income / Assets

(3) Residual Income = Operating income – cost of capital
   a. Cost of capital = the "imputed" interest on the assets used to generate the income.
(4) Return on equity(ROE) = Net income / Equity

(5) Return on sales = Net Income / Equity

(6) Sales @ Margin of Safety = Margin of safety sales + Breakeven sales

(7) Breakeven sales = Fixed Costs / Contribution margin ratio

(8) Contribution Margin Ratio = Contribution margin / Sales

(9) Breakeven units = total FC / (Price/unit - VC/unit)

5.14 Questions and Answers

For more multiple-choice questions and answers visit http://cpa.suryapadhi.com/

5.14.1 Question

Wren Co. manufactures and sells two products with selling prices and variable costs as follows:

	A	B
Selling price	$18.00	$22.00
Variable costs	12.00	14.00

Wren's total annual fixed costs are $38,400. Wren sells four units of A for every unit of B. If operating income last year was $28,800, what was the number of units Wren sold?

a) 5,486
b) 6,000
c) 9,600
d) 10,500

Answer is D

For every 5 products sold (4 units of A and 1 unit of B) Wren's contribution margin is $32 [($18 × 4 + $22) – ($12 × 4 + $14)]. To produce a profit of $28,800 with fixed costs of $38,400, Wren must sell 2,100 [($28,800 desired profit + $38,400 fixed costs) ÷ $32)] sets of 5 products. Wren must sell 10,500 (2,100 sets × 5 products per set) total products.

5.14.2 Question

Yeager Corporation has used **regression analysis** to perform price elasticity analysis. In doing so management regressed the quantity demanded (y variable) against price (x variable) with the following results:

Multiple R	.86798
Adjusted R squared	.72458
Standard error	542.33
Intercept	56400.50
Price coefficient	– 4598.20

Calculate the predicted quantity demanded if price is set at $7.00.

a) 24,213
b) 88,588
c) 31,234
d) 18,454

Answer is A

The formula is Quantity demanded = a + bx = 56,400.50 + (7.00 × – 4,598.2) = 24,213.

5.14.3 Question

The following information is available for Armstrong Enterprises for 2012:

Net operating income after taxes	$36,000,000
Depreciation expense	15,000,000
Change in net working capital (increase)	10,000,000
Capital expenditures	12,000,000
Invested capital (net assets)	100,000,000
Weighted average cost of capital	10%

What is the free cash flow for 2012?

a) 36,000,000

b) 30,000,000

c) 29,000,000

d) 26,000,000

Answer is C

Free cash flow is calculated as follows:

Net operating income after taxes	$36,000,000
+Depreciation expense	15,000,000
−Change in net working capital	(10,000,000)
−Capital expenditures	(12,000,000)
= Free cash flow	$29,000,000

5.14.4 Question

A manufacturing company employs a process cost system. The company's product passes through both Department 1 and Department 2 in order to be completed. Conversion costs are incurred uniformly throughout the process in Department 2. The direct material is added in Department 2 when conversion is 80% complete. This direct material is a preservative that does not change the volume. Spoiled units are discovered at the final inspection and are recognized then for costing purposes. The physical flow of units for the current month is presented below.

Beginning work in process in Department 2 (90% complete with respect to conversion costs)	14,000
Transferred in from Department 1	76,000
Completed and transferred to finished goods	80,000
Spoiled units—all normal	1,500
Ending work in process in Department 2 (60% complete with respect to conversion costs)	8,500

If the manufacturing company uses the FIFO (first-in, first-out) method, the equivalent units for conversion costs in Department 2 for the current month would be

a) 72,500

b) 74,000

c) 85,200

d) 86,600

Answer is B

This answer is correct. This response uses the correct calculations.

Supporting Calculations

Physical schedule

Units to account for:		
Beginning WIP	14,000	
Trans-in Dept. 1	76,000	
Total units to account for	90,000	
Units accounted for:		
Units completed (80,000)		
From beginning WIP (90%)	14,000	1,400
From current production	66,000	66,000
(80,000 – 14,000)		
Total units completed	80,000	
Spoiled	1,500	1,500
Ending WIP (60%)	8,500	5,100
Total units accounted for	90,000	74,000

Or

	Units	Completion Factors	Equivalent Units
Completed	80000	1.00	80,000.00
Beginning WIP (completed in last period)	14000	-0.90	(12,600.00)
Ending WIP	8500	0.60	5,100.00
			72,500.00
Add Spoiled	1500	1	1,500.00
			74,000.00

5.14.5 Question

Black, Inc. employs a weighted average method in its process costing system. Black's work in process inventory on June 30 consists of 40,000 units. These units are 100% complete with respect to materials and 60% complete with respect to conversion costs. The equivalent unit costs are $5.00 for materials and $7.00 for conversion costs. What is the total cost of the June 30 work in process inventory?

A. $200,000
B. $288,000

C. $480,000

D. $368,000

Explanation

Choice "d" is Correct and is computed in the following computation. The information provided by this question simply requires you to convert total production to equivalent units and multiply those units by the equivalent unit costs.

	Material		Conversion Cost		Total
WIP @ Jun 30	40000		40000		
% of completion	100%		60%		
Equivalent Unit	40000		24000		
Cost	$ 5.00	$	7.00		
Total	$ 200,000.00	$	168,000.00	$	368,000.00

5.14.6 Question

Feline Fabrications produces two products, Me and Ow, with joint production costs of $60,000. The company elects to use the net realizable value method of allocating costs between the 15,000 units of Me and 30,000 units of Ow produced during the year ended December 31, Year 1. Me has a selling price after split-off of $4.00 and separable costs of $30,000 while Ow has a selling price after split-off of $3.00 and separable costs after split-off of $20,000. What joint production costs will be allocated to each product?

    Me   Ow

A. $20,000 $40,000

B. $18,000 $42,000

C. $36,000 $24,000

D. $30,000 $30,000

Explanation

Choice "b" is correct. The net realizable value method allocates joint costs based upon the ratio of each product's net realizable value as follows:

	Product Me	Product Ow	Total
Selling price	4	3	
Unit Produced	15000	30000	
Total Sales value	60000	90000	150000
Less Separable Cost	30000	20000	
Net Realizable value @ split off point	30000	70000	100000
Percentage of Total	30%	70%	100%

Total Joint cost			60000
Joint cost by product	18000	42000	600000

5.14.7 Question

Mighty, Inc. processes chickens for distribution to major grocery chains. The two major products resulting from the production process are white breast meat and legs. Joint costs of $600,000 are incurred during standard production runs each month, which produce a total of 100,000 pounds of white breast meat and 50,000 pounds of legs. Each pound of white breast meat sells for $2 and each pound of legs sells for $1. If there are no further processing costs incurred after the split-off point, what amount of the joint costs could be allocated to the white breast meat on a relative sales value basis?

- A. $120,000
- B. $200,000
- C. $480,000
- D. $400,000

Explanation

Joint costs allocated based upon relative sales value at split off are allocated based upon the ratio of individual sales values to sales value at split off. The ratio is computed at 80% and 20% and applied to the $600,000 in joint cost to arrive at the joint cost allocation below. Be careful of the question. This question asks for the amount of allocated joint costs, but others may ask for total costs. In those instances, you would add the allocated costs to the direct costs that can be traced to the product prior to split off

	Pounds	Price Pound	Sales Value Split off	Relative value	Joint cost	Joint Cost Allocation
White breast meat	100,000	$2.00	$ 200,000.00	80%	$ 600,000.00	$ 480,000.00
Legs	50,000	$1.00	$ 50,000.00	20%		$ 120,000.00
T			$ 250,000.00	100%		$ 600,000.00

Choice "c" is correct.

5.14.8 Question

Lucy Sportswear manufactures a specialty line of T-shirts using a job order cost system. During March, the following costs were incurred in completing Job ICU2: direct materials $13,700; direct labor $4,800; administrative $1,400; and selling $5,600. Factory overhead was applied at the rate of $25 per machine hour, and Job ICU2 required 800 machine hours. If Job ICU2 resulted in 7,000 good shirts, the cost of goods sold per unit would be:

A. $5.70
B. $6.00
C. $6.50
D. $5.50

Explanation

Job ICU2 Costs	Total Cost	Good Units		Unit Cost	
Direct materials	$13,700				
Direct labor	$4,800				
Factory overhead 800 hrs	$20,000				
Total mfg	$38,500	÷ 7,000	=	$5.50	D
Selling	$5,600				
Administrative	$1,400				
Total cost	$45,500	÷ 7,000	=	$6.50	Not A

Choice "d" is correct. $5.50 cost of goods sold ($38, 500 ÷ 7,000 units).

5.14.9 Question

Kimbeth Manufacturing uses a process cost system to manufacture Dust Density Sensors for the mining industry. The following information pertains to operations for the month of May:

	Units
Beginning work-in-process inventory, May 1	16000
Started in production during May	100,000
Completed production during May	92000
Ending work-in-process inventory, May 31	24000

The beginning inventory was 60 percent complete for materials and 20 percent complete for conversion costs. The ending inventory was 90 percent complete for materials and 40 percent complete for conversion costs.

Costs pertaining to the month of May are as follows:

- Beginning inventory costs are: materials, $54,560; direct labor $20,320; and factory overhead, $15,240.
- Costs incurred during May are: materials used, $468,000; direct labor, $182,880; and factory overhead, $391,160.

Using the weighted-average method, the equivalent unit cost of materials for May is:

a. $4.60

b. $5.46

c. $5.03

d. $4.50

Explanation

	Actual Units	Completed	Equiv. Units	Total Cost	Unit Cost	
Beginning Inventory	16,000	60%	9,600	$54,560		
Add: Started	100,000	SQZ	104,000	468,000	$4.50	FIFO
Total Available	116,000		113,600	522,560	$4.60	Weighted Average
Less: Completed	-92,000	100%	-92,000			
Ending Inventory	24,000	90%	21,600	$97,200	$ 4,50	FIFO

Or,

	Actual Units	% Completed during the current period	FIFO	Weighted Average
Beginning Inventory	16,000	40%	6400	
Completed	92,000	100%	92,000	92,000
Less Beginning Inventory (included in	-16000	100%	-16,000	
Ending Inventory	24,000	90%	21,600	21,600
Total Units			104,000	113,600
Cost for calculation			Only current cost 468,000	Beg + Curr $54,560 +468,000
Cost per Unit			4.5	4.6

Choice "a" is correct. $4.60 equivalent unit cost of materials using the weighted-average method ($54,560 beg. inv. + $468,000 additions = $522,560 ÷ 113,600 total avail. equivalent units).

FORMULAS

6   Formulas

6.1   Standard Costing Variance Analysis

Ratios	Formula	Purpose
Material price variance	SRAQ – ARAQ, Or A.Qty (S. Rate – A. Rate). Actual and standard price times the actual quantity purchased	Direct Material Price Variance is the difference between the actual cost of direct material and the standard cost of quantity purchased or consumed.
Material usage variance	SRSQ – SRAQ, Or S. Rate (S.Qty – A.Qty) Actual and standard usage times X the standard price.	Direct Material Usage Variance is the measure of difference between the actual quantity of material utilized during a period and the standard consumption of material for the level of output achieved.
Total material variance	SRSQ – ARAQ, Or Price variance + Usage variance.	
Labor rate (price) variance	SRAH – ARAH, Or A.Hrs (S.Rate – A.Rate Actual and standard price times the actual number of hours worked. =	Direct Labor Rate Variance is the measure of difference between the actual cost of direct labor and the standard cost of direct labor utilized during a period.
The labor efficiency (usage) variance	SRAH – SRAH, Or S.Rate (S.Hrs. – A. Hrs.) Difference between actual and standard number of hours	Direct Labor Efficiency Variance is the measure of difference between the standard cost of actual number of direct labor hours utilized during a period and the standard hours of direct labor for the level of output achieved.

	times the standard rate (price). *The standard number of hours is the amount that should have been used for the quantity actually made.*	
Total labor variance	Rate variance + Efficiency variance.	
The variable overhead efficiency variance	SRSH – SRAH, Or SR (SHrs – AHrs) Difference between actual hours worked and the flexible budget hours times the standard variable overhead rate per hour.	Variable Overhead Efficiency Variance is the measure of impact on the standard variable overheads due to the difference between standard number of manufacturing hours and the actual hours worked during the period.
The variable overhead (OH) spending variance	SRAH – ARAH, Or AHrs (SR-AR) Difference between actual variable overhead spending and budgeted variable overhead costs based upon actual hours worked.	Variable Overhead Spending Variance is the difference between variable production overhead expense incurred during a period and the standard variable overhead expenditure. The variance is also referred to as variable overhead rate variance and variable overhead expenditure variance.
The fixed overhead budget (spending) variance	Actual fixed cost – budgeted fixed cost. Difference between actual fixed overhead and budgeted fixed overhead.	Fixed Overhead Expenditure Variance, also known as fixed overhead spending variance, is the difference between budgeted and actual fixed production overheads during a period
The fixed overhead volume variance	Difference between the applied fixed	Fixed Manufacturing Overhead Volume Variance quantifies the difference between budgeted and absorbed fixed production overheads.

	overhead cost and the budgeted fixed overhead cost.

6.2   Turnover Ratios

Ratios	Formula	Purpose
Remember TSA, **T**urnover = **S**ales(numerator) divided by **A**verage (denominator)		
Account Receivable Turnover	Net Credit Sales ÷ Average Net Account receivables.	Indicates the receivable quality & the success of the company in collecting o/s receivable. Faster turnover gives credibility to the current & acid test ratios
Account Payable Turnover	Cost of Goods Sold ÷ Average Net Account Payables	Accounts payable turnover is a ratio that measures the speed with which a company pays its suppliers. If the turnover ratio declines from one period to the next, this indicates that the company is paying its suppliers more slowly, and may be an indicator of worsening financial condition.
Inventory Turn Over	Cost of Goods Sold ÷ Average Inventory	This measures of how quickly inventory is sold is an indicator of co. performance. The higher the turnover in gen, the better the performance
Total Assets Turn Over	Net Sales ÷ Average Total Assets	Asset turnover ratio is the ratio of the value of a company's sales or revenues generated relative to the value of its assets. The Asset Turnover ratio can often be used as an indicator of the efficiency with which a company is deploying its assets in generating revenue.
Investment Turnover	Net sales ÷ Average Invested Capital (Long Term Liabilities + Equity)	The investment turnover ratio compares the revenues produced by a business to its debt and equity. The ratio is used to evaluate the ability of a management team to generate revenue with a specific amount of funding..
Working Capital Turnover	Net Sales ÷ Average working capital	Working capital turnover ratio is an activity ratio that measures dollars of revenue generated per dollar of investment in working capital
1) Numerator is always sales except for AP & Inventory (COGS)		
2) Denominator is average of the name of the formula. Average = (Beginning Balance + End Balance) /2		

Ratios	Formula	Purpose

AVERAGE TURNOVER IN DAYS -Just reverse the turnover ratio and divide the denominator by 365

Accounts Receivable Turnover in days Or Days sales outstanding Or Accounts Receivable Collection Period	Average Accounts Receivable / (Net Credit sales / 365) Or 365 /Account receivable Turnover Or Average Account receivable / daily credit sales	Indicates the average numbers of days required to collect A/R; the more he sales are o/s. the longer the receivable is o/s
Inventory Turnover in Days	Average inventory / (Cost of Goods Sold / 365) Or 365 / Inventory Turnover Or, Average Inventory / daily cost of goods sold	Indicates the average no. of days required to sell inventory.
Accounts Payable Turnover in days. Or Account Receivable Deferral Period	Average Accounts Payable / (Cost of Goods Sold / 365) Or 365 / Account Payable Turnover Or, Average Accounts Receivable / daily cost of goods sold.	

6.3 Cash Cycle

Ratios	Formula	Purpose
Operating Cycle	Accounts receivable Turnover in Days + Inventory Turnover in Days	The operating cycle is the average period of time required for a business to make an initial outlay of cash to produce goods, sell the goods, and receive cash from customers in exchange for the goods.
Cash Conversion Cycle	Accounts receivable Turnover in Days + Inventory Turnover in Days – Accounts Payable Turnover	The cash conversion cycle is a metric used to gauge the effectiveness of a company's management and, consequently, the overall health of that company. The calculation measures how fast a company can convert cash on hand into inventory and accounts payable, through sales and accounts receivable, and then back into cash
Annual Percentage Rate (APR) of	(365 / (Payment Period – Discount	

Quick Payment Discount	Period)) X (Discount / (100 % - Discount %))	

6.4 Profitability Ratios

Ratios	Formula	Purpose
RETURN - same formula as "TURNOVER" but instead of sales in the numerator, use net income		
Remember RNA, Return = NI(numerator) divided by Average(denominator)		
Return of Total Assets (ROA)	NI / Average Total Assets	A profitability ratio that produces a % output making it easy to compare companies that differ in sizes
Return on Investment	NI + Interest (1-tax rate) / Capital (Long Term Liability + Equity)	Measures co.'s % return relative to its capital investment risk without regard to the method of financing (Income over Invested Capital)
Return on Equity (ROE)	NI / Total Equity	a critical measure for determining a co.'s effectiveness; measure of the rate of return earned by a company on the equity component of its capital structure.
Return on Common Equity (ROE)	(NI – Preferred Dividend) / Average Common Equity	
Profit Margin	NI / Sales	Measures the operating efficiency
Financial Leverage or, degree of financial leverage (DFL).	Average Total Assets / Equity	Is defined as the degree to w/c a firm's use of debt to finance the firm magnifies the effects of a given % change in EBIT on the % change in EPS
Operating Leverage or, degree of operating leverages (DOL)	Contribution Margin / Net Operating Income	Operating leverage is a measurement of the degree to which a firm or project incurs a combination of fixed and variable costs.
Total Leverage or, Degree of Total leverage.	Degree of Financial Leverage * degree of Operating leverage.	
Dupont Return on Assets	Profit Margin X Total Assets Turnover	this ratio allows for increased analysis of changes in the percentages. The net profit margin indicates the percent return on each sale while the asset turnover indicates the effective use of

		assets in generating that sale.
Dupont Return on Equity	Profit Margin X Assets Turnover X Financial Leverage	is defined as the degree to w/c a firm's use of debt to finance the firm magnifies th effects of a given % change in EBIT on the % change in EPS

6.5 Liquidity Ratios

Ratios	Formula	Purpose
Quick Acid Test Ratio	Liquid Current Assets / Current Liabilities. * Inventory & prepaid expenses are not considered as liquid asset.	used in working capital analysis to evaluate firm's short-term liquidity; ability to meet current obligation w/o liquidating its inventory
Current Ratio, Working Capital Ratio	Current Assets / Current Liabilities	Measures the no, of times CA exceed CL and way of measuring short-term solvency and also shows ability of the firm to generate cash to meets its short-term.
Debt to Equity	Total Liabilities / Common Equity	Indicates the degree of protection to creditors in case of solvency. The lower this ration the better the co. position.
Debt ratio aka Debt-to-Assets ratio	Total Liabilities /Total Assets	the ratio indicates how much of the total assets are financed by the creditors
Debt-to-total-capital ratio	Total debt / Total Capital (Debt + Equity)	measure of financial leverage; the ratio provides indication related to org's LT debt-paying ability, the lower the ratio, the > the level of solvency and the greater the presumed ability to pay debts
Operating Cash flow to total debt	Operating Cash Flow / Total Debt	
Time Interest earned	Earnings before interest and taxed (EBIT) / Interest expense	the ratio reflects the ability of a company to cover interest charges. It uses income bef interest and taxes to reflect the amt of income available to cover interest expense
Cost of factoring	Net cost/average amount invested	
Asset base	Working capital + PPE	
Hurdle Rate		A hurdle rate is the minimum rate of return on a project or investment required by a manager or investor. The

		hurdle rate denotes appropriate compensation for the level of risk present; riskier projects generally have higher hurdle rates than those that are deemed to be less risky.
Hurdle Income	Asset base x Imputed interest rate	
Total target income	Hurdle income + Residual income target (given)	

6.6 Cost of capital

Ratios	Formula	Purpose
Cost of equity capital(R_e)	(Expected dividend / Current share price) + Growth rate	
Cost of Equity (as Capital Assets Pricing Model) CAPM Model	Risk free rate + Risk premium. =Risk-free rate + Beta (LT average risk premium for the market - Risk-free rate). $RF + B(RR - RF)$ Beta = Measures correlation between stock's price + price of the overall market.	
Cost of Debt (R_d)	Interest rate (1- tax rate)	Cost of debt refers to the effective rate a company pays on its current debt. In most cases, this phrase refers to after-tax cost of debt, but it also refers to a company's cost of debt before taking taxes into account.
Cost of preferred stock (R_{ps})	Preferred Dividend / Net issue price Net Issue Price = Face Value – Floating cost _ Discount + Premium	

6.7 Economic Indicators

Ratios	Formula
Gross Domestic Product Expenditure approach	**GICE** **G**overnment Purchases + Gross Domestic **I**nvestment + Personal **C**onsumption + Net **E**xports
Gross Domestic Product Income approach	**PAID RITE** Corporate **P**rofits + **A**djustment for Net Foreign Income + net **I**nterest + **D**epreciation + **R**ental Income + **I**ncome of Proprietor + Indirect Business **T**axes + **E**mployee Compensation
Net National Product (NNP)	GNP - Deprecation
Net Domestic Product (NDP)	GDP - Depreciation
National Income (NI)	NNP – Indirect Business Taxes
Personal Income(PI)	Household and non-corporate business incomes
Disposal Income(DI)	PI – Personal Taxes

6.8   Unemployment

Ratios	Formula	Purpose
Unemployment Rate	Number of Employment ÷ Total Labor Force X 100	

6.9   Inflation

Ratios	Formula	Purpose
Inflation Rate	(CPI current Period - CPI of last period) / CPI of last period X 100	
Real GDP	Normal GDP / GDP Deflator X 100	

6.10 Process Costing

Ratios	Formula	Purpose	
Equivalent Unit - FIFO	Unit Completed		XXX.XX
	Add Ending WIP X % Completed		XXX.XX
	Less – Beginning WIP X % completed (earlier period)		(XXXX.XX)
			=======
	Equivalent Units		XXX.XX
Cost Equivalent Unit – FIFO	= Current cost / Equivalent units		
	Under the FIFO, only the costs incurred in current period are allocated between finished goods and ending work-in-process (WIP) because FIFO maintains beginning inventory costs that are completely separate from current-period costs.		
Equivalent Unit – Weighted Average	Unit Completed	XXX.XX	
	Add Ending WIP X % Completed	XXX.XX	
		=======	
	Equivalent Units	XXX.XX	
Cost Equivalent Unit – Weighted Average	= (Beginning cost + current cost) / Equivalent units		
	In weighted-average all materials and all processing (conversion) costs (both those incurred this period and those in Beginning WIP).		

6.11 Breakeven Analysis

Ratios	Formula Purpose
Cost of Goods Manufactured (COGM)	DL + DM + OH applied
Contribution Margin	Sales Price – Variable Cost
Contribution Margin Ratio	Contribution margin / Sales
Breakeven Point in Units	Fixed cost / contribution margin
Breakeven Point in $	Fixed cost / contribution margin ratio
Required Sales	(Fixed cost + target profit) / contribution margin
Margin of Safety (MS)	Total Sales in $ - Breakeven Sales in $
	Excess of budgeted sales over BE volume of sales; measures the amount by which sales can drop before losses begin to incur
MS %	MS$ / Total sales

6.12   Direct Costing

Ratios	Formula	Purpose
Fixed Cost	Total Cost – Variable Cost	
High / Low method Variable Cost	= (Cost at high – cost at low) / (activities at high – activities at low)	

6.13   Others Financial Formulas

Ratios	Formula	Purpose
Regression Analysis	Y = A + B(X), Total Cost = Fixed Cost + Variable Rate (Units)	
Economic Value Added	Income After Taxes – (Weighted average cost of capital X (Long Term Liability + Equity)) Economic value added is simply the net operating profit after tax, less the cost of financing the company's capital. Calculate economic value added by multiplying the invested capital by its weighted-average cost of capital	
Residual Income	Income after Tax - (Desired rate of return X Assets)	
Bank Deposit Reserve Ratio	= Reserve / Total demand	
EOQ	$\sqrt{\dfrac{2DO}{C}}$ or $\sqrt{\dfrac{2AP}{S}}$ = A, D= annual demand P, O=cost to place an order S, C=cost to store inventory	
Average carrying cost of inventory	Average Inventory X Cost per Unit X Cost of Capital	
Payback Period (In terms of Year)	Initial Investment / Annual cash flow	
IRR (PV factor)	Investment ÷ Annual cash flow	
ARR(ROI)	Accounting Income ÷ Average investment	
Return on Investment (ROI)	Net Income ÷ Investment	
ROA (Return on Assets)	Net Income ÷ Average Total Assets	

ROE (Return on Equity)	(Net Income – Preference Dividend) ÷ Average Common Equity
Price earnings ratio	Market Price of Stock ÷ EPS
Present value for any single future payment	Payment ÷ $(1 + R)^n$
Percentage changes for account balances for Year 1 to Year 2	(Current balance – Prior Balance) ÷ Prior Balance
Profitability Index (PI)	$\dfrac{\text{Present value of Cash flow}}{\text{Initial Investment}}$
Taxable Income	Sales – Operating expenses – Tax Deprecation
After-tax income	Taxable Income x (1-tax rate)
Cash coverage	(EBIT + Depreciation) ÷ Interest
Gross Margin Ratio	Gross Margin ÷ Net Sales Revenue
Gross Margin	Sales – COGS (Cost of Goods Sold)

6.14 Others Non -Financial Ratios

Ratios	Formula		
Price Elasticity of Demand	% Change in Quantity demanded ÷ % change in price Change in Demand = New Quantity – Old Quantity / OLD Quantity Change in price = New Quantity – Old Quantity / OLD Quantity		
	Ed > 1	Elastic demand	Price ↑: Qd↓: TR ↓
	Ed < 1	Inelastic demand	Price ↑: Qd Δ little: TR ↑
	ED = 1	Unitary	
		QD – Quantity demanded, TR = Total revenue	
Income Elasticity of demand	= (% change in QD) ÷ (% change in Income)		
	Ed > 0	Normal good	Income ↑: Qd ↑
	Ed < 1	Inferior good	Income ↑: Qd ↓

Cross-elasticity of demand	= (% Δ in QD of x) /(% Δ in $ of Y)		
	Ed > 0	Substitute	Price Y ↑: Qd X ↑
	Ed < 1	Complement	Price X ↑: Qd Y ↓

MEMORY AID

Ratios	Mnemonics	Descriptions
Factors that shift the demand curve	WRTTEN	W- Wealth R – Related goods price I - Income of consumers T – Taste of consumers or preferences E – Expectation of Consumers N –Number of Buyer served by market
Factors that shift the SUPPLY curve	ECOST	E- Expectation of price of the supplier C- Cost of production O – Price / demand of Other goods T - Technology of the product
Six Sigma – Existing Product / Business process Improvement	DMAIC	D- Define Problem M – Measure Key Aspects of current problem A – Analyze data I – Improve / Optimize current processes C – Control
Six Sigma – new product / Business process Development	DMADV	D- Define Problem M – Measure Key Aspects of current problem A – Analyze data D – Design V – Verify

FLASH CARD

Glossary	Descriptions
Absolute Conformance	**Absolute conformance** represents perfect compliance with pre-established levels of quality. Absolute conformance is the most rigorous standard of quality because it represents a perfect, or ideal, level of compliance.
Absorption cost	Absorption costs represent an accounting for resources used that are usually consistent with generally accepted accounting principles and include fixed costs that frequently do not change with the selection of different alternates. When production is greater than sales, absorption costing income is greater than variable costing income. Production in excess of sales result in increases in inventory that include capitalization of fixed product costs that are immediately expensed under variable costing. Since costs that are used in the determination of net income for variable costing are accounted for in inventory for absorption costing, absorption costing will produce higher net income than variable costing when production is greater than sales. Absorption costs are not relevant in situations when management must decide on accepting or rejecting one-time-only special orders, and where there is enough idle capacity.
Account analysis	The account analysis method is merely a review of all the accounts by someone knowledgeable of the activities of the firm. It is only as good as the person making the judgments.
Accounting Information system	An accounting information system is a subsystem within a management information system. An AIS deals with accounting transactions. It is a part of **an** MIS.
Accounting rate of return	Accounting rate of return is based on accrual income rather than cash flows. It does not consider the time value of money and is considered inferior to the discounted cash flow methods. = Average Annual Income ÷ Initial Investment
Activity Based Costing	Activity-based costing is an accounting system that collects financial and operating data based on the underlying nature and extent of the cost drivers. Activity-based costing focuses on value added by identifying the cost drivers that add value. Activity-based costing focuses on the cost of activities and seeks to only invest resources in value added activity.
Ad hoc report	An ad hoc report demands without having to get a software developer involved.
Analytical processing	Analytical processing allows end users to retrieve data from a system and perform analysis using statistical and graphical tools. Remote analysis is not

	synonymous with remote processing.
Application programmers	Application programmers is the person responsible for writing and/or maintaining application programs and should not be responsible for controlling or handling data. responsible for also controlling or handling data.
Authority certificate	**Authority certificate** may be a transposition of certificate authority, the group which issues encrypted digital certificates containing a public key.
Backdoor	A backdoor is a means of access to a program or system that bypasses normal security procedures.
Balance of power	The concept of balance of power anticipates that no one nation will dominate or interfere with the activities of others.
Balanced scorecard	The balanced scorecard reports management information regarding organizational Financial and non-financial performance as defined by "critical success factors." These critical success factors are often classified as 1. F - Financial solvency and return, 2. I - Internal business processes, 3. C - Customer satisfaction, 4. H - Human resource innovation to demonstrate that no single dimension of organizational performance can be relied upon to evaluate success. Critical success factors identified in the balanced scorecard generally include human resource aspects, particularly as it relates to harnessing employee innovation, internal business process improvement, customer satisfaction, and financial performance.
Batch processing	With a batch processing, input documents / transactions are collected and grouped by type of transaction. These groups (called batches) are processed periodically (e.g., daily, weekly, monthly, etc.).
Batch totals	Batch totals are used with all batches of transactions as they are entered. Batch totals can be used on dollar amounts even when the transactions are entered online. However, batch totals are not used on fields such as account numbers. If totals of account numbers (or any other non-dollar mounts) are used for batches of transactions, they are called hash totals.
Benchmarking	Benchmarks represent the best practices within an industry or within a function. They may serve as the individual standards that serve to evaluate the achievement of goals classified within the context of critical success factors but they are not, themselves, the features that an organization must possess to accomplish their strategy. Benchmarking relates to determining best practices and, often, using those practices as standards.
Bonds	Bonds are debt instruments that require specific fixed payments, mature at a specific time and increase debt. Immediately after issue, increases in debt increase the debt equity ratio and decrease credit worthiness.
Break-even analysis	Break-even analysis assumes that all variable costs and revenues are constant on a per unit basis and are linear over a relevant range. Fixed costs in total are constant.
Business Cycle	The business cycle is the rise and fall of economic activity relative to its long-term

growth trend.

The sequence of a typical business cycle includes
- an expansionary phase
- a peak of economic activity,
- a contractionary phase – and
- a trough of economic activity.

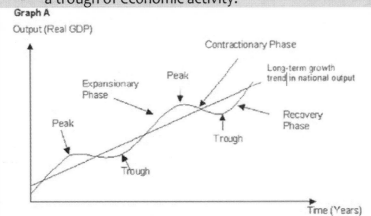

During a contraction or a recession, most industries experience a decline in sales and profits. Similarly, during an expansion, most industries experience an increase in sales and profits.

Business process management	**Business process management** seeks incremental change by tweaking the existing process and design. Business process management decreases financial risk associated with change because the change is incremental and made to an already functioning process. If it goes badly, you will still be left with a process that works.
Business process reengineering	Business process reengineering seeks radical change by ignoring the current process and instead starts from the beginning to design a different way of achieving the end goal and/or product. Business process reengineering has a longer implementation time because it involves radical change.
Call Option	Call options would allow, but not require, the purchaser of the call to acquire the currency for a specified price at or before a specified time in the future. If the price goes up, the option holder would exercise the options; if not, the option holder would adopt market rate and let the options expire. Used in case of Account payable
Callable bond	Callable bonds would fluctuate in value. In fact, one of the advantages to the issuer of callable bonds is the ability to call or, effectively, refinance the bonds if interest rates become favorable
Capital Assets Pricing model	Capital Asset Pricing Model (CAPM) Cost of Capital = R + B (M - R) Where C = Cost of capital R = Risk free rate B = Beta M = Market rate of return
Capital Budgeting	Capital budgeting involves the management's evaluation of an uncertain future. Management's decisions on the increased requirement for capital

	investment and the required return and the cost of capital require evaluation of an uncertain future can estimated with the help of capital budgeting.
Centralized processing	Centralized processing environments maintain all data and perform all data processing at a central location. Processing is not performed at remote locations.
Check digits	Check digits can be effective on the entry of some numeric fields such as account numbers (and can be used with account numbers that are not totally numeric) that must follow a specific pattern. Check digits are not effective on the entry of dollar amounts since dollar amounts do not follow a specific pattern.
COBIT	The COBIT framework identifies seven information criteria (ICE RACE) that include Integrity, Confidentiality, Efficiency, Reliability, Availability, Compliance and Effectiveness. The COBIT Framework includes four domains in the mnemonic **PO AIDS ME:** Mnemonic Purpose PO Process and Organize Direct the IT Process **AI** Acquire and Implement Deliver the IT <u>Solution</u> **DS** Deliver and Support Deliver the IT Service **ME** Monitor and Evaluate Ensure directions are followed
Coefficient of determination	The coefficient of determination measures the proportion of the total variation in "y" or total cost that is explained by the total variation in the independent variable, x, or variable costs. The coefficient of determination measures the reliability of the formula, but is not used for determining the value of "y". The standard error (also standard error of the mean) is a measurement used in conjunction with standard deviation computations and is not relevant to this projection.
Collection Period	The average collection period for a firm measures the number of days after a typical credit sale is made until the firm receives the payment. Average collection period will be decreased due to a change in credit policy because of 1. Increase in sales, 2. Increase in discounts taken, 3. Decrease in the amount of bad debt, and 4. Decrease in the investment in accounts receivable.
Collusive pricing	Collusive pricing anticipates that competitors will collude or conspire to maintain prices and mutual profitability. Collusive pricing undermines competitive pricing and maintains prices to external customers at levels higher than they would be in a competitive marketplace.
Common stock	Common stock is an equity security that conveys ownership. Common stock does not require any payment, it does not mature and, because it

	increases equity while having no effect on debt, it decreases the debt equity ratio and increases the creditworthiness of the firm.
Compensating balances	Compensating balance is a bank requirement. The bank will require a certain balance be maintained in cash. This amount cannot be used for working capital purposes.
Complementary goods.	Two goods are complements if they are used together or their demand curves move together (breakfast cereal and milk, e.g., or tennis balls and tennis racquets). Thus, if the price of one complement goes up, demand for the other good goes down. A rise in the price of a complementary commodity would cause a shift to the left in any demand cure (representing decrease in demand, at all price levels, for that product). With respect to complementary goods, the demand for the primary product is directly impacted by the demand (and hence the price changes) for the complementary goods.
Complementary goods	Complementary goods are ones whose demand fluctuates together. If Good A and Good B are complements, then if the demand for Good A increases, the demand for Good B will also increase, tennis rackets and tennis balls are complements.
Complementary goods	The demands for mutually "complementary goods" fluctuate together (e.g., more cereal purchases are accompanied by an increase in the demand for milk).
Computer Operator	A computer operator is responsible for scheduling processing jobs, etc., and would not have actual custody of the data. Effectively the operator is in a recordkeeping function that should be segregated from custody.
Computer programmer	A computer programmer may be either an application programmer responsible for writing or maintaining application programs or a system programmer responsible for installing supporting monitoring and maintaining the operating system. Programmers have a recordkeeping function that should be segregated from the librarian's custody function.
Concentration banking	Concentration banking automatically channels funds from every source of the business into a single usable account, thus quickly identifying available funds each day, and moving them to accounts that have funding requirements that day, and investing the remainder in short-term, interest-bearing instruments until needed.
Conforming costs	Conforming costs are those preventative and appraisal costs invested to detect and prevent errors and do not represent quality standards.
Consumer price index	The CPI is a measure of the overall cost of a fixed basket of goods and services purchased by an average household. It is primarily used to compare relative price changes over time. The consumer price index is a measure of the inflation rate (the percentage change of the consumer price index from one period to the next). it is only one measure of inflation; there are others, such as the producers price index, but the consumer price index is the most widely known and used.
Continuous probability	Continuous probability simulation is a procedure that studies a problem by creating a model of the process and then, through trial and error solutions,

	attempts to improve the problem solution.
Continuous quality improvement	Continuous quality improvement represents an unswerving focus on customer satisfaction and quality. It is not necessary that continuous quality improvement the specific steps associated with value chain analysis.
Contraction / recession phase of business cycle	When potential national income (potential Gross Domestic Product, also referred to as the Long Run Aggregate Supply) is greater than the achieved national income, the short run aggregate supply curve is shifting to the left indicating a contraction or recession.
Control Chart	Control charts measure conformance of operations within a standard range known as a goalpost (an upper or lower limit).
Convertible bonds	Convertible bonds would fluctuate in value. In fact, one of the advantages to the investor (and potentially the issuer) in relation to convertible bonds is the ability to covert or, effectively, swap the bonds for equity if market conditions become favorable (equity returns exceed fixed return on debt).
Cost (Push) inflation	Cost (Push) inflation is inflation caused by a shift left in aggregate supply. For example, A sharp increase in the price of oil, will cause the short-run aggregate supply curve to shift left and thus increase the aggregate price level causing inflation.
Cost leadership	Cost leadership focused on a broad range of buyers would emphasize price to a large number of buyers, not by various features.
Cost of discount forgone	The cost of lost discounts is the product of the number of interim periods within a year represented by the credit period extended after the discount period times the effective rate of interest for that period, which is computed as the discount percentage divided by the net amount due within the discount period (also expressed as a percentage). Cost of discount forgone = Discount % / (100-Discount %) x (360/Allowed payment days – Discount days)
Cost of Product	In microeconomic analysis, in the long run all supply side inputs are variable. In accounting terms, this means that in the long run all costs are variable. (e.g., the fixed cost of depreciation of a factory building becomes a variable cost when a second factory building is added.)
Cost-volume profit analysis	Cost-volume profit analysis is a method used to evaluate operating decisions.
CRM	CRM systems provide sales force automation and customer services. CRM systems record and manage customer contacts, manage salespeople, forecast sales and sales targets and goals, manage sales leads and potential sales leads, provide and manage online quotes and product specifications and pricing, and analyze sales data. This statement is correct. The objectives of CRM systems are to increase customer satisfaction and customer revenue.
Cross elasticity	The cross elasticity of demand is an economic concept that measures the responsiveness in the quantity demanded of one good when the price for another good changes. Also called cross-price elasticity of demand, this measurement is calculated by taking the percentage change in the quantity demanded of one good and dividing it by the percentage change in the price of

	the other good.

Cross Price Elasticity of Demand Formula $= \dfrac{(\Delta Q_X / Q_X)}{(\Delta P_Y / P_Y)}$

Cyclical unemployment	Cyclical unemployment is due to a downturn (recession) in the economy which leads to a decline in real GDP and higher unemployment.
Cyclical unemployment	
Data Librarian	A **Data librarian** is the most appropriate position to maintain custody of an entity's data. As the name implies the librarian maintains custody of the "library" of data generated by an organization.
Data mining	Data mining refers to the process of sifting through large amounts of data, impossible to analyze by individuals, to search for relationships amongst various data as a means for achieving strategic or competitive advantage. Data mining can be defined as the extraction of implicit, previously unknown, and potentially useful information from data. It is usually associated with an organization's need to identify trends. Data mining invokes the process of analyzing the data to show patterns or relationships in that data. Thus, pattern recognition, or the ability of the data mining software to recognize the pattern (or trends), is the critical success factor for data mining (at least in the opinion of the Examiners).
Data warehouse	A data warehouse is an enterprise-wide database that stores data that has been extracted from various operational and external databases from within the organization. The data in these data warehouses has been gathered and combined from several sources into this main central location.
Database Marketing	Database marketing involves gathering information on customers and using the information from that database to segment customers into target markets for a more effective selling effort.
Debt covenant	A debt covenant is a provision in a bond or debt indenture (contract between the bond issuer and the bond holders) that the bond /debt issuer will either do (affirmative covenants) or not do (negative covenants) certain things.
Decentralized (distributed) processing	Decentralized (distributed) processing numerous remote platforms rather than a central computer or processor.
Decision support systems	Decision support systems are computer-based information systems that provide interactive support to managers or others during the decision-making process.
Default risk	Default risk is the risk that the security will not be repaid because the issuing entity is insolvent or illiquid.
Deflation	Deflation is a general decline in the overall price level (i.e., when the inflation rate is negative). Increasing the money supply causes the overall price level to rise. As a result, it helps eliminate deflation.
Delphi method	The Delphi method of forecasting involves the use of multiple teams in geographically remote locations. Information is shared and gathered in a central

	point and compiled and then redistributed for comment. The method is highly interpersonal and requires significant judgment.
Demand Curve	The demand curve illustrates the maximum quantity of a specific good that consumers are willing and able to purchase at each and every price, all else being equal. Thus, the demand curve reflects the impact that price has on the amount of a product purchased. - A decline in interest rates would cause the aggregate demand curve to shift right, which increases real GDP. - A decline in input costs would cause the aggregate supply curve to shift right, which also increases real GDP.
Demand Report	A demand report is a specific report that can be printed or viewed on demand.
Denial of service attack	In a denial of service attack, one computer bombards another computer with a flood of information intended to keep legitimate users from accessing the target computer or network. A sudden surge of false requests that cause a company's server to crash is a denial of service attack. A denial-of-service attack is an attack in which one computer bombards another computer with a flood of information intended to keep legitimate users from accessing the target computer or network.
Differentiation	Differentiation focused on a narrow range (niche) of buyers would differentiate the product within the context of a very few buyers and might specifically emphasize one feature such as prestige (for the status conscious professional), performance (for the auto enthusiast), or safety for families, etc.
Digital encryption	Digital encryption refers generically to the encoding of messages and does not contemplate the specific mechanisms used to transmit information across the internet from remote locations.
Digital signature	A digital signature is a means of ensuring that a message is not altered in transmission. It is a form of data encryption.
Direct Costing	Direct costing (more accurately called variable or marginal costing) capitalizes only the variable production costs (direct materials, direct labor, and variable overhead) to inventory (product costs), while fixed costs are expensed as period cost.
Direct Labor	Direct labor represents the cost of labor directly associated with the manufacturing of the finished product.
Discount Rate	The discount or hurdle rate is determined in advance for computations of net present value. Project cash flows are discounted based upon a predetermined rate and compared to the investment in the project to arrive at a positive or negative net present value. Advance determination of management's required return is integral to the development and evaluation of net present value.
Disposable income	Disposable income is computed as personal income (the income received by households and noncorporate businesses) net of personal taxes. Disposable income is the amount left over from personal income that is available either to spend or save.
Distributed database	A distributed database is a database that is distributed in some manner on different pieces of either local or remote hardware via an Intranet or Extranet. The various pieces of the database may be distributed world wide or on some smaller geographic area.

Dual Pricing	Dual pricing invokes appropriately assigning different prices to the same product in different market settings. Dual pricing is a sophisticated extension of competitive pricing. The prices are simply established at the levels appropriate for each market and would not result in higher prices than would be experienced in competitive markets.
Eavesdropping attack	An eavesdropping attack seeks to access a network and steal or eavesdrop on communications in an attempt to illicitly obtain passwords or other confidential or sensitive information.
Economic Order Quantity	Economic order quantity (EOQ) is an inventory model that attempts to minimize both ordering and carrying costs. The objective of the EOQ is to compute the quantity to order. EOQ = square root (2SO/ C) Where: EOQ = Order size S = Annual Sales quantity in units O = Cost per purchase Order C = Annual cost of Carrying one unit in stock for one year
Economic value added	Economic value added is a residual income measure that compares income with required return on investment. Positive amounts indicate objectives have been met, negative amounts indicate that objectives have not been met. The method does not equate investment cash outflows and cash inflows. Economic value-added is a residual income technique used for capital budgeting and performance evaluation. It represents the residual (excess) income of project earnings in excess of the cost of capital (including cost of equity) associated with invested capital.
Economies of scale	In the long run, a firm may experience increasing returns due to economies of scale which come into full play only if a large enough number of units is being produced to make it worthwhile to set up a fairly elaborate productive organization.
Effective performance	Effective performance measures have a number of characteristics. They should relate to the goals of organization, be objective and easily measured, be under the control of the employee, and understood by the employees. Contribution to the goals of the organization is a characteristic of an effective performance measure
Elasticity of Demand	Demand is elastic if a decline in price (P) results in an increase in total revenue (TR); or if an increase in P results in a decline in TR. On the other hand, if demand is inelastic, a decline in P will result in a decline in TR or an increase in P will result in an increase in TR. - A price elasticity of demand of 2.0 means demand will change by 2x (as a percentage) for any change in price. This is called elastic. - Perfectly elastic demand does not exist. - Perfectly inelastic demand means the quantity demanded will not change when price changes.

	- Inelastic demand responds less than 1x (as a percentage) for a change in price.
Elasticity of supply	Price elasticity of supply is calculated the same way as demand except that quantity supplied is measured: Price elasticity <u>Change in quantity supplied</u> of supply (%) change in price Perfectly inelastic supply curves are also vertical representing that supply is insensitive to changes in price; i.e., the quantity supplied will not change as price changes.
Electronic data interchange (EDI)	Electronic data interchange (EDI) (intercompany exchange of computer-processable business information) requires strict adherence to a standard data format. Translation software is required to convert internal company data to this format. EDI requires that companies have a prior relationship. Agreements will have been drawn up between the companies to outline how the systems will operate.
E-Marketing	E-marketing uses the internet to accomplish marketing functions.
End users	End users are any workers who enter data into a system or use the information processed by the system. End users could be secretaries, administrators, accountants, auditors, CEOs, and so on.
Engineering method	The engineering method uses such methods as time and motion study to classify costs, It can only be used where there is an observable relationship between the inputs and the outputs.
Engineering standards	The best basis for setting standards is engineering standards based on attainable performance. Tight standards are good, but if unattainable, employees will not be motivated.
Enterprise Resource Planning	An enterprise resource planning system is a cross-functional enterprise system that integrates and automates the many business processes that must work together in the manufacturing, logistics, distribution, accounting, finance, and human resource functions of a business. Enterprise Resource Planning (ERP) coordinates information to ensure timely and responsive reporting and data administration in support of decisions.
Equilibrium	Intersection of demand curve and supply curve is called Equiibrium

Government price regulations in competitive markets that set

- maximum or ceiling prices below the equilibrium price will create shortages
- minimum or floor prices above the equilibrium price will create surplus

Exception Report	An exception report is a report produced when a specific condition or "exception" occurs.
Executive steering committee.	Approving project deliverables is a responsibility of the executive steering committee.
Expansionary monetary	Expansionary monetary policy results when the Fed increases the money supply. Expansionary monetary policy affects the economy through the following chain of events: (1) an increase in the money supply causes interest rates to fall, (2) falling interest rates stimulate the desired levels of firm investment and household consumption, (3) increases in desired investment and consumption cause an increase in aggregate demand, and (4) aggregate demand shifts to the right causing real GDP and the price level to rise.
Contraction policy	Under contraction policy, the Federal Reserve would most likely - Raising the discount rate will dampen the economy. - Raising the reserve requirement will dampen the economy, because there will be less money to loan.
Expansionary policy	Under an expansionary policy, the Federal Reserve would most likely - purchase government securities. Purchasing these securities increases the money supply and expands the economy. - Reducing the reserve requirement will expand the economy, not dampen it, because there will be more money to loan - -Reduce the interest rate, it charges to its member bank. Under contraction policy, the Federal Reserve would most likely - Raising the discount rate will dampen the economy. - Raising the reserve requirement will dampen the economy, because

	there will be less money to loan.
Expected value	Expected value computations that assign probabilities to potential outcomes quantify both the likelihood (percentage) and outcome (amounts) into a single value. Expected value is therefore the most useful of the listed statistics when risk is being prioritized. Probability and **expected value**. The course of action with the highest expected monetary value should be selected.
eXtensible Business Reporting Language	XBRL, the acronym for eXtensible Business Reporting Language, is derived from MIL (eXtensible markup language). XBRL is an open, royalty-free, Internet-based information standard for business reporting of all kinds. XBRL labels data so that they are provided with context that remains with them and brings conformity to the names by which they are recognized by disparate software.
Extranets	Extranets are networks that directly link certain intranets of an organization with other organizations or individuals with which the organization may have a relationship. Extranets can enable customers, vendors, suppliers, consultants, subcontractors, and others to gain access to certain areas of a private intranet.
Federal bank discount rate	The Federal bank discount rate refers to the rate established by the Federal Reserve for short-term loans it makes to member banks.
Financial Risks	Financial risk is a general category of risk that includes: • Interest rate risk -> Interest rate risk is the fluctuation in the value of a "financial asset" when interest rates change. • Market risk • Purchasing power risk -> Purchasing power risk is the risk that price levels will change and affect asset values (mostly real estate). • Liquidity risk -> Liquidity risk is associated with the ability to sell the temporary investment in a short period of time without significant price concessions • Default risk -> Financial risk, also called default risk, relates to the exposure of lenders to the failure of borrowers to repay principal and interest on debt. An entity using its own cumulative earnings in capitalizing its operations is not exposed to default risk. • Business risk represents the risk associated with the unique circumstances of a particular company, as they might affect the shareholder value of that company. If an entity purely uses its own cumulative earnings in capitalizing its operations, it is exposed to the risks of its own unique circumstances.
Firewall	A firewall is an "electronic device" (a firewall may actually be both hardware and software and not just hardware) that prevents unauthorized users from gaining access to network resources. A firewall isolates a private network of some type from a public network (or a network segment from the main network). It also maintains a (controlled) connection between those two networks.
Fiscal Policy	Policy of the government to counter inflation or deflation. The policy can be a Expansionary policy or a contraction policy

	Increase in Money Supply (Expansionary policy) - If the Federal Reserve buy U.S. Treasury bonds, that would increase the money supply. - Decreasing reserve requirements would mean more lending because banks would have to hold a small portion of amounts deposited in reserve. - If the Federal Reserve wanted to increase the money supply, it would reduce the discount rate. A lower discount rate would reduce short-term interest rates, which would encourage more (short-term) borrowing at the lower interest rate (lower cost means more demand). More borrowing means more lending and more money in the economy. **Decrease in Money Supply (contraction policy)** - Selling more U.S. Treasury bonds would reduce the money supply since the bonds would have to be paid for with money out of the money supply. - Increasing reserve requirements would mean less lending because banks would have to hold a larger portion of amounts deposited in reserve.
Fishbone	Cause and effect (fishbone) diagrams typically analyze problems that contribute to the occurrence of defects.
Floating-rate bonds	Floating-rate bonds would automatically adjust the return on a financial instrument to produce a constant market value for that instrument. No premium or discount would be required since market changes would be accounted for through the interest rate.
Foreign trade zone	A foreign trade zone contemplates a physical location in which tariffs are waived on imported products until they leave the zone. Foreign trade zones anticipate delay rather than reductions in tariffs.
Frictional unemployment	Frictional unemployment is the unemployment that arises from workers routinely changing jobs or from workers being temporarily laid off. It results from the time needed to match qualified job seekers with available jobs.
Gap analysis	Gap analysis determines the difference between industry best practices and current company practices. It focuses on quality as it identifies areas that need improvement to meet industry best practices.
Globalization	Globalization is the distribution of industrial and service activities across an increasing number of nations. Globalization does not describe the actions of a single company. Globalization represents the increased dispersion and integration of the world's economies. Globalization is often objectively measured as the growth in world trade as a percentage of GDP.
Goalpost	Goalpost conformance assumes a range of acceptable results. Because it represents achievement of compliance within an established range of tolerable error, goalpost conformance is considered less rigorous than absolute

	conformance.
Gross Domestic Product	Gross domestic product (GDP) is the total dollar (monetary) value of all new final products and services produced **within the economy** in a given time period. The emphasis is on the final goods and services. The expenditure approach to computing GDP includes exports and other components included in the mnemonic "GICE": 1. Government expenditures 2. Capital investment 3. Consumption 4. *Net exports*
Hierarchy of data	The hierarchy of data in a system begins with the smallest component of data and ends with the most summarized. A **character** is a symbol such as a letter or number. A field is a collection of numbers or letters such as a name or a street address. A **record** is a group of fields such as a customer name and address and related accounts receivable amount. A **file** is a collection of records such as an account receivable subsidiary ledger.
High Low Method	The high-low method is a simplified approach that uses only the points of highest and lowest activity. The regression method considers every point of activity
Historical cost	Historical cost is generally not relevant in a decision analysis situation.
Incentive to hold inventory.	The amount of inventory that a company would tend to hold in stock would increase as the: a. Variability of sales decreases. b. Cost of running out of stock decreases. c. Length of time that goods are in transit decreases.
Incremental backup	An incremental backup in which copying only the data items that have changed since the last backup. This produces a set of incremental backup files, each containing the results of one day's transactions.
Inferior good	An inferior good is one for which the demand declines as income increases. A normal good would experience an increase in demand in response to an increase in income. Because the demand for hamburger went down as income increased, it is an inferior good.
Input routine	An input routine is a series of steps in a program to ensure the accuracy of entered data. It might include steps such as limit tests, field checks, validity tests, etc.
Interest rate risk	Interest rate risk is the fluctuation in the value of a "financial asset" when interest rates change.
Interest rate swap agreement	An **interest rate swap agreement** would be effective in hedging the risk associated with interest rate fluctuations. A swap agreement is a private agreement between two parties, generally assisted by an intermediary, to exchange future cash payments. In case of swap agreement, one party enters into agreement with another party a fixed rate of interest in exchange for receipt of payments of a floating rate of interest.
Internal costs	Internal costs analysis includes analyzing the internal value-creating ability of a

analysis	firm, so the sources of profit and costs of the internal activities of the firm must be analyzed.
Internal Failure Cost	In a quality control program, internal failure costs are incurred because nonconforming products and services are detected prior to being shipped to customers. Examples are rework, scrap, re-inspection and retesting
Internal rate of return	Internal rate of return (IRR) determines the compound interest rate of an investment where the present value of the cash inflows equals the present value of the cash outflows. The IRR is the discount rate that results in a net present value of zero. The internal rate of return (IRR) method is less reliable than the net present value (NPV) technique when there are several alternating periods of net cash inflows and net cash outflows or the amounts of cash flows differ significantly. The IRR is strictly a percentage measure of return, while the NPV is an absolute measure. Due to this difference, the timing or amount of cash flows under IRR can be misleading when compared to the NPV method.
Internet	The Internet is a tremendous number of servers dedicated to sending and receiving information to and from other networks. It is comprised of hundreds of thousands of business, government, military and education networks around the world that all communicate with each other.
Intranets	Intranets are private networks that people outside of an organization generally have no access to. Intranets share organizational information by connecting geographically separate LANs within an organization.
Job Control Language	Job Control Language is something associated with IBM mainframes, specifically batch processing applications. Job Control Language, which can be almost as complex as any programming language, is used to "interface" between the jobs that are to be run and the operating system. Jobs normally consist of multiple programs to be run, and the Job Control Language controls the running of the jobs and programs. It also allows the programs to be written somewhat generically, and the Job Control Language makes the translation, for example, from the generic file names used in the programs (INPUTFILE) and the specific files names (ACCOUNTSRECEIVABLEMASTER) and version names that are actually to be used when the job is run.
Just in Time	Just-in-time management emphasizes efficiency by scheduling the deployment of resources just-in-time to meet customer or production requirements. Characteristics - specialize in merely one job or task. Specialize in merely one job or task. - coordination of supplies inventory with synchronization of production scheduling with demand and supplies arrive at regular intervals throughout the production day. - Reduced set up times that no longer need to accommodate buffers for delivery of goods are benefits and features of just-in-time inventory systems. - Just-in-time requires a sense of empowerment amongst employees to ensure the coordination of production and materials delivery is handled with maximum efficiency and accommodates variable schedules.

Kaizen	**Kaizen**, or continuous improvement, occurs at the manufacturing stage where the ongoing search for cost reductions takes the form of analysis of production processes to ensure that resource uses stay within target costs.
Law of diminishing returns	The law of diminishing returns states that an increase in labor or capital beyond a certain point causes a less-than-proportionate increase in production.
Lean manufacturing	Lean manufacturing or lean production emphasizes the use of only those resources required to meet the requirements of customers. It is somewhat like activity-based approaches, as it seeks to invest resources only in value-added activities. The main objective in lean manufacturing is waste reduction. Although customer requirements and demand-pull serve as the basis for the approach, quality is not the preeminent concept.
Learning curve	Learning curve analysis is used to determine increases in efficiency or production as experience is gained. Both products have long production runs, making learning curve analysis the best method for estimating the cost of the competitive bid.
Liquidity risk	Liquidity risk is associated with the ability to sell the temporary investment in a short period of time without significant price concessions.
Local area network (LAN)	A local area network (LAN) is a computer network that connects computers of all sizes, workstations, terminals, and other devices within a limited proximity.
Lockbox system	A lockbox system expedites cash inflows (minimizes collection float) by having a bank receive payments from a company's customers directly, via mailboxes to which the bank has access. Payments that arrive in these mailboxes are deposited into the company's account immediately. Lockboxes are systems of mailboxes, usually in many locations, where customers send payments. The company's bank checks these mailboxes frequently and immediately deposits checks received. This accelerates the collection of accounts receivable.
Long-term debt	Long-term debt requires specific fixed payments, includes maturity at a specific time and (by definition), increases debt. Immediately after issue, increases in debt increase the debt equity ratio and decrease credit worthiness.
Loop verification	Loop verification is the process of confirming the correctness of the entered data by displaying additional information after data has been entered
Market value added	Market value added contemplates the degree to which management's actions improve stockholder value. It does not specifically identify multiple dimensions of business performance.
Master Budget	A master budget is an overall budget, consisting of many smaller budgets, that is based on one specific level of production. A flexible budget is a series of budgets based on different activity levels within the relevant range.
Materials requirements planning (MRP)	Materials requirements planning (MRP) is an inventory management technique that projects and plans inventory levels in order to control the usage of raw materials in the production process. MRP primarily applies to work in process and raw materials
Monopolistic competition	A market with many independent firms, low barriers to entry, and product differentiation is best classified as monopolistic competition to entry and firms

	exert some influence over price in such a market. Best examples are brand name consumer products price in such a market. Best examples are brand name consumer products.
Monopoly	When there are few good substitutes for a suppliers product, the supplier has market power (think of a monopoly). As a result, the supplier is better able to control buyers and act as a price setter rather than a price taker.
Motive to hold cash	There are three primary motives for holding cash: 1. Transactions demand 2. Precautionary demand 3. Speculative demand
Multilateral	Multilateral refers to power that is not only distributed but shared cooperatively among nations.
Multiple regression analysis	Multiple regression analysis is an expansion of simple regression because it allows consideration of more than one independent variable. The other elements are consistent in simple and multiple regression analysis.
Multipolar	Power distributed amongst multiple nations refers to a multipolar distribution of power.
Multiprocessing	Multiprocessing, not multiprogramming, is the coordinated processing of programs by more than one processor. In multiprocessing, several programs are run at the same time.
Multiprogramming	Multi-programming not multiprocessing, is several parts of a program running at the same time on a single processor. In multiprogramming, since there is only one processor, only one part of a program can actually run at a single point in time. Multiprogramming takes advantage of a wait state with one program (where the program is waiting for something else like relatively slow input/output) to switch to another program.
Natural unemployment	The natural unemployment rate is the sum of frictional, structural, and seasonal unemployment or the unemployment rate that exists when the economy reaches its potential output.
Net Present Value	The net present value is the difference between the cost of an investment and the present value of its cash flows. If the net present value of a project is positive, it would indicate that the rate of return for the project is greater than the discount percentage rate (hurdle rate) used in the net present value computation. When using the net present value method of capital budgeting, different hurdle rates can be used for each year of the project. The net present value (NPV) method of capital expenditure evaluation does not provide the true rate of return on investment. The NPV indicates whether or not an investment will earn the "hurdle rate" used in the NPV calculation. If the NPV is positive, the return on investment will exceed the hurdle rate. If the NPV is negative, the return on investment will be less than the hurdle rate. If the NPV is zero, the return on investment will be exactly equal to the hurdle rate.
Network Marketing	Network marketing, sometimes referred to as multilevel marketing, focuses on relationships and referrals to accomplish marketing functions.
Non-conformance	Rework – is a internal failure costs, a subset of nonconformance costs.

costs	Rework of products assumes errors are caught and corrected before delivery. Reduction of rework is an indication of improved efficiency and product quality. Product returns create nonconformance costs and external failure costs. Warranty expense is a nonconformance cost, it is an external failure cost, not an internal failure cost. Nonconforming costs are those internal and external failures associated with correcting quality errors associated with non-compliance and do not represent quality standards
Normalization	Normalization is the process of separating data into logical tables. Data normalization is required before a relational database can be designed.
Object-oriented databases	Object-oriented databases can be used to store comments, drawings, images, voice, and video that do not normally fit into more structured databases. However, object-oriented databases are normally slower than, not faster than, relational databases.
Offshore operations	Offshore operations are the outsourcing of services or business functions to an external party in a different country.
Online – Realtime processing	With OLRT processing, transactions are entered, and the master files updated as the transactions are entered.
Online Analytical processing	Online analytical processing allows end users to retrieve data from a system and perform analysis using statistical and graphical tools.
Online processing	Method in which each transaction goes through all processing steps (data entry, data validation, and master file update) before the next transaction is processed. OLRT files are always current, and error detection is immediate. OLRT files are always current, and error detection is immediate.
Operating budgets	Operating budgets describe the plan for revenue and expenses and the supporting schedules that go with them. Examples include sales, materials, labor, overhead, production, purchases and the forecasting of cash that will be necessary to pay for them. Capital budgets plan for the purchase of capital assets, which will only affect the operating budget through their subsequent effect on expense via depreciation.
Operating leverage	Operating leverage is the presence of fixed costs in operations, which allows a small change in sales to produce a larger relative change in profits. Degree of operating leverage= Profit divided Contribution margin.
Opportunity cost	Opportunity cost is the next best use of productive capacity. The production that is forfeited to produce the special order is referred to as the next best alterative use of the facility. Opportunity costs are costs that would have been saved or profits that would have been earned if another decision alternative had been selected.
Ordinary Annuity	Annuity due factor for cash inflows are received at the end of the year. The annuity due factor would be used if the cash inflows were received at the beginning of each year.
Outsourcing	Non-core functions to one business become critical for companies providing

	outsourcing services thereby reducing risk exposure in the event an issue arises. Disadvantages of Outsourcing a. Language barriers. b. Security issues. c. Quality of service.
Parallel count	A parallel count appears to be the counting of bits in a parallel fashion. It appears to have something to do with digital circuits in digital clocks, watches, microwave ovens, VCRs, and the like. It is not a computer program.
Parallel processing	In **parallel processing**, there are multiple processors that share the execution of an individual program; the program is split into pieces and the multiple pieces of the single program are run concurrently by the multiple processors. This capability will benefit programs that are mitten to take advantage of it.
Pareto Chart	Pareto diagrams combine the elements of a histogram of quality control issues displayed in order of most to least frequent with a line graph that displays the cumulative occurrence of the problems.
Payback period	The payback method determines the number of years that it will take for a company to recoup or be paid back for its investment. The payback method does not consider the time value of money. The payback method neglects total project profitability. It simply looks at the time required to recover the initial investment; subsequent cash flows are ignored. Payback and bailout payback do not consider the time value of money or the return after the initial investment is recovered. The difference between the two methods is that bailout payback takes salvage value into account in calculating cash flows.
Peak	A peak is the highest point of economic activity. It is the point where real GDP is at its highest level in the cycle and unemployment is at its lowest level in the cycle.
Perfect Competition	Factors of Perfect Competition, increase the bargaining power of the customer, these are: - Customers make up a large volume of a fine's business. - There is much information available to customers. - The buyers have low switching costs. - There are a high number - The market is not growing fast. - There are several equal-sized firms in the market. - Customers do not have strong brand preferences. - The costs of exiting the market exceed the costs of continuing to operate. - Some firms profit from making certain moves to increase market share. - The various firms in the market use different types of strategic plans.

Perfectly inelastic	When a good is demanded, no matter the price, demand is described as perfectly inelastic. The demand "curve" is a vertical line at the quantity demand with price making no difference
Period Cost	Period costs are costs that are expensed during a period. They are not charged to a product (capitalized), which is why they are expensed.
Personal income tax	An increase in the personal income tax will cause a decrease in aggregate demand (i.e., causes the aggregate demand cure to shift left). As a result, an increase in taxes causes real GDP to fall and unemployment to rise.
PERT	PERT is a technique used in project management that focuses on the time required to complete each step in a project. It allows a project manager to monitor a projects progress and identify potential bottlenecks or delays that will postpone the completion date.
Phishing	Phishing is the sending of phony emails to try to convince people to divulge information like account numbers and social security numbers. It is often accomplished by luring people to authentic looking but fake websites
Piggybacking	Piggybacking is the practice of using another person or organization's wireless network connection without the express permission of the subscriber or owner of the network.
Portfolio Theory	Portfolio theory is concerned with construction of an investment portfolio that efficiently balances its risk with its rate of return. Risk is often reduced by diversification, the process of mixing investments of different or offsetting risks. The broad categories of risk are summarized in the following mnemonic to get us DUNS. • **Unsystematic (non-market/firm-specific) / Diversifiable** - Diversifiable risk can be eliminated through effective application of portfolio theory. Diversifiable risks are also termed unsystematic risk. • **Non-diversifiable / Systematic (market)** - Non-diversifiable risk cannot be eliminated by the application of portfolio theory. Non-diversifiable risk is also referred to as market or systematic risk.
Predatory pricing strategies	Predatory pricing strategies typically result in lower prices to external customers than competitive pricing. Predatory pricing (below market or even below cost) is undertaken by larger organizations that can absorb losses and deliberately do so in an attempt to break smaller, less capitalized, competitors from the marketplace
Prime Rate of interest	The prime rate of interest represents the rate offered by banks to their most credit worthy debtors. The prime rate of return would not necessarily consider the risk-specific return required for a particular company's IRR and would not be appropriate as a hurdle rate.
Principle of comparative advantage	The principle of comparative advantage states that even if one of two regions is absolutely more efficient in the production of every good than is the other, if each region specializes in the products in which it has a comparative advantage (greatest relative efficiency), trade will be mutually profitable to both regions. Real wages of productive factors will rise in both places. This principle is the basis for international trade.
Principle of	The principle of substitution states that people tend to shift their buying

substitution	from relatively expensive to relatively cheap goods. Thus, if the price of a product falls, people tend to buy more of it and less of other (relatively) more expensive products.
Processing power	Processing power is often measured in terms of MIPS, which is millions of instructions per second, not per minute.
Product cost	Product (inventoriable) costs include direct labor, direct material, and applied overhead. Direct material costs anticipate a provision for normal spoilage. Sales commissions are selling and administrative expenses that are period (not product) costs, and abnormal spoilage is charged against income of the period as a separate component of cost of goods sold. Product cost is assigned to goods (products) that were either purchased or manufactured for resale.
Profitability index	The profitability index is the ratio of the present value of net future cash inflows to the present value of the net initial investment. The profitability index is also referred to as the *"excess present value index"* or simply the "present value index." Companies hope that this ratio will be over 1.0, which means that the present value of the inflows is greater than the present value of the outflows. $$\text{Profitability index} = \frac{\text{Present value of net future cash inflows}}{\text{Present value of net initial investment}}$$ The profitability index is the ratio of the present value of net future cash inflows to the present value of the net initial investment. The profitability ratio requires detailed long-term forecasts of project's cash flows. For longer term projects, cash flow projections might be either unavailable or unreliable
Program flow chart	A program flowchart is a diagrammatic representation of the sequence of processing steps and the logic included in a computer program.
Program modification controls.	Program modification controls are controls over the modification of programs being used in production applications. Program modification controls include both controls that attempt to prevent changes by unauthorized personnel and also that track program changes so that there is an exact record of what versions of what programs were running in production at any specific point in time. Program change control software normally includes a software change management tool and a change request tracking tool.
Project Manager	Responsibility for - Project administration on a day-to-day basis including identifying Managing intimal and external stakeholder expectations.
Project members.	Carrying out the work and producing the deliverables is a responsibility of the project members.
Project sponsor	The project sponsor is an individual at the executive level of management

	who is responsible for allocation of fund and resources to the project. The role of the project sponsor includes responsibility for overall project delivery. Interfacing between the organization and the project itself is a responsibility of the project sponsor.
Put Option	Put options would allow, but not require, the purchaser of the put to sell the currency for a specified price at a specified time in the future. Used in case of Account receivable
Quality Cost	Quality cost is divided into two categories (1) Conformation cost -> cost incurred to conform the product to quality, Further sub-divided into (1) preventive cost and (2) Appraisal cost (2) Non-conformation cost – Cost incurred due to con conformation product (1) Internal cost and (2) External cost. • Prevention -> Cost incurred to prevent from happening -> Preventive maintenance, Redesign of processes • Appraisal -> Cost incurred to detect the defects, Examples of these cost are, Testing, Statistical quality checks, Inspections, Testing, Maintenance of lab • Internal failure -> Cost intercurred to correct the defect and these costs are incurred before sending the product to customer -> Tooling changes • External failure -> Cost incurred to correct the error to fix the defect detected by customer -> Responding to customer complaints is an external failure cost incurred because products or services failed to conform to requirements alter being delivered to customers. An increase in conformance costs (prevention and appraisal) resulted in a higher quality product and a decrease in non-conformance costs (internal and external failure costs).
Real GDP per capita	Real GDP per capita is real GDP divided by population. Real GDP per capita is typically used to compare standards of living across countries or across time. By dividing real GDP by population, this measure adjusts for differences in the size of countries and for differences in population over time.
Recession	A recession is defined as a period of falling GDP and rising unemployment. GDP will fall if there is a decrease in aggregate demand or a decrease in aggregate supply.
Regression analysis	Regression analysis is a statistical model that can estimate the dependent cost variable based on changes in the independent variable. Regression analysis is a statistical method that fits a line to the data by the method of least squares. It is the most accurate way to classify costs of an object as either fixed or variable.

Relational database	In a relational database, the data are stored in two-dimensional tables that are related to each other by keys, not implemented by indexes and linked lists. Indexes and linked lists were normally used in the earlier hierarchical and tree-structured databases.
Relative Sales Value	Sales price less the cost to complete is defined as the relative sales value at split-off. In other words, this is the additional contribution to income generated by completing the product.
Relevance	Relevance defines that quality of data and information that makes a difference in decision making. Relevance has the greatest impact on management's ability to make effective decisions.
Relevant Cost	Relevant costs are costs that are relevant to a particular decision. The relevance of a particular cost to a decision is determined by potential effect on the decision. Relevant costs are expected future costs that vary, with the action taken. When considering alternative, such as discontinuation of a product line, management should consider relevant costs. Relevant costs are those costs that will change under different alternative. Residual income is the segment margin of an investment center after deducting the imputed interest (hurdle rate) on the assets used by the investment center.
Residual income	Residual income methods (including economic value added) focus on target return and amount and encourage managers to invest in projects that exceed the hurdle rate. As a result, divisions with high rates of return do not fear dilution of their rates and are not discouraged from making investments that demonstrate strong residual income performance.
Restricted Stock	Restricted stock option programs may reward current performance but also emphasize future performance. The employee must typically stay through the option strike period and the option is only valuable if the stock price increases.
Return on investment (ROI)	Return on investment (ROI) measures may discourage mangers from avoiding investments that could benefit the company as a whole. Use of the ROI exclusively as a measure of performance can inadvertently focus managers purely on maximizing short-term returns. Profitable units are reluctant to invest in additional productive resources because their short-term result will be to reduce ROI.
Risk averse behavior	Risk averse behavior occurs when an investors risk < expected rate of return. The investor seeks higher returns for more risk.
Risk Behavior	**Risk averse behavior** describes managers who demand more return on an investment as risk increases. These managers expect to be compensated for increased risk. **Risk seeking behavior** describes managers who seek reduced return for higher risk.

	Risk indifferent behavior describes a manager who is neutral with regard to the return associated with a particular investment. Typically, the amount of a risk-free rate of return associated with an investment of a given amount compared to a higher return associated with higher risk is viewed as having equal value.
Risk indifferent behavior	Risk indifferent behavior occurs when an investor's risk = expected return on the investment Risk indifferent behavior describes a manager who is neutral with regard to the return associated with a particular investment. Typically, the amount of a risk free rate of return associated with an investment of a given amount compared to a higher return associated with higher risk is viewed as having equal value.
Risk Premium	- **Default risk premium (DRP)** is the additional compensation demanded by lenders for bearing the risk that the issuer of the security will fail to pay interest or fail to repay the principal. - **Purchasing power risk premium, or inflation premium (IP)**, is the compensation investors require to bear the risk that price levels may change and affect asset values or the purchasing power of invested dollars (e.g., real estate). - **Maturity risk premium (MRP)**, or interest rate risk, is the compensation investors demand for bearing risk. This risk increases with the term to maturity.
Risk seeking behavior	Risk seeking behavior occurs when an investors risk > expected rate of return. The investor seeks higher returns for more risk.
Safety Stock	Safety stock levels are affected by: 1. Uncertain sales forecasts - greater uncertainty means a higher level of safety stock should be carried. 2. Dissatisfaction of customers - if customers are dissatisfied with back orders (which occur when there are stock outs), then more safety stock should be carried to prevent stock outs. 3. Uncertain lead times - greater uncertainty means a higher level of safety stock is needed.
Scatter graph	The scatter graph method is used in statistical analysis to plot relationships between variables to determine a line function that best describes those relationships.
Scheduled reports	Scheduled reports are the more traditional reports that display information in a predefined format and that are made available on a regular basis.
SCOR mode	The SCOR model includes a series of processes or steps defined as plan, source, make, and deliver. Plan - The process of planning consists of developing a way to properly balance aggregate demand and aggregate supply within the goals and objectives of the firm and plan for the necessary infrastructure. The process of planning consists of developing a way to properly balance aggregate demand and aggregate supply within the goals and objectives of the firm and plan for the necessary infrastructure. Assessing the ability of the

	suppliers to supply resources is part of the "plan" process.
	Source - Selecting vendors is a source decision, not a plan decision. Selecting vendors is a "source" step that implements that plan.
	Once demand has been planned, it is necessary to procure the resources required to meet it and to manage the infrastructure that exists for the sources. Collecting and processing vendor payments falls into the "source" process.
	Make - The "make" process encompasses all the activities that turn the raw materials into finished products that are produced to meet a planned demand. Implementing changes in the engineering process falls into the "make" process
	Deliver - The "deliver" process encompasses all the activities of getting the finished product into the hands of the ultimate consumers to meet their planned demand. Managing accounts receivable and collections from customers falls into the "deliver" process
Sequential file	Sequential file processing is almost totally restricted to batch processing. Sequential file processing was used extensively in the "good old days" but it is seldom used these days for major application files, which are almost always disk files and allow direct access. Tapes (which are the normal sequential files) are normally restricted to backups and storage for very large amounts of data that are too expensive to be stored on disk and for which there is no real need for relatively quick access.
Shared services	Shared services would involve splitting the cost of a service with another organization, not contracting out with a separate entity.
Short term unemployment.	Short term unemployment is a broad description that relates to the duration of an unemployment condition. The duration of unemployment can be caused by any number of factors, however, structural influences such as technological advancement that require workforce retraining would likely not be short term.
Short-term debt	Short-term debt requires specific fixed payments, includes maturity at a specific time and, by definition, increase debt. Immediately after issue, increases in debt increase the debt equity ratio and decrease credit worthiness.
Six Sigma	Six Sigma emphasizes cost reduction above production constraints.
Software developer	A software developer designs and/or writes the systems and/or programs to collect, process, store, transform and distribute the data and information that are entered by the end users.
Sourcing	Sourcing requirements generally refer to content or value added limits on the percentage of labor or materials used in imported products. Compliance with limits may result in tariff reductions.
Spoofing attack	A spoofing attack is a breach of network security resulting from a person or program successfully impersonating a legitimate network user for illegitimate purposes.
Standards	Standards imposed by management without employee input are referred to

	as authoritative standards..
	Standards developed in collaboration with employees involved with the work are referred to as participative standards.
	Ideal standards are based on optimum condition.
	Attainable standards represent per unit budgets that assume normal conditions.
Structural unemployment	Technological advances would likely result in structural unemployment. Structural unemployment is characterized by available jobs that do not match the skill sets of the workforce. Technological advances could create jobs that simultaneously make the skills of the workforce obsolete.
	Structural unemployment occurs when the jobs available do not match the skills of the unemployed individuals or when the individuals do not live where jobs are available with their skills.
Structured system	A structured system is a system in which each program within a system is independent of other programs within the system. This enables programming teams to work independently on different programs within the same system.
Substitute goods	For substitute goods, as the price of one good goes up, the demand for another, substitute good increases as consumers desire the lower-priced substitute good.
Superior goods	Just as the demand for inferior goods declines with an increase in the income level of a consumer, superior goods will experience a spurt in demand as prices are raised.
Supply and Demand Shift	When the supply of and demand for a good both increase, equilibrium quantity increases. However, the impact on price is indeterminate. If demand and supply increase by the same amount, price will remain unchanged. However, if demand increases by more than supply, price will increase. Conversely, if supply increases by more than demand, price will decrease.
Supply Curve	The supply curve measures the maximum quantity of a specific good that sellers are willing and able to produce at each and every price.
Supply Curve	The movement of points along the supply curve, represents a change in quantity supplied as a result of a change in price and is the measure of a willingness of producers to offer a product at alternative prices.
SWOT Analysis	Evaluation of internal and external factors contributing to an organization's success is referred to as Strengths, Weaknesses, Opportunities and Threats (SWOT) analysis. Strengths and weaknesses focus on internal factors while opportunities and threats relate to external factors.
System Analyst	A systems analyst is the position that designs the overall application system. The systems analyst has, effectively, an authorization role that should be segregated from the custody role.
Theory of constraints	The theory of constraints is concerned with maximizing throughput by identifying and alleviating constraints.
	The theory of constraints says that organizations are impeded from achieving

	objectives by the existence of one or more constraints. Organizations or projects must be operated in a manner that either works around or leverages the constraint (in this case, the bottleneck).
Theory of economies of scale	The theory of economies of scale states that, as a production process gets larger, the process becomes more efficient and productivity increases. The theory of diminishing return is the opposite of economies of scale in that it holds that, as more product is produced, the factory gets less productivity out of its workforce and machinery. Factors contributing to economies of scale include: • Labor specialization • Managerial specialization • Utilization of by products (or joint products) • Efficient use of capital equipment • Volume discount purchasing
Throughput cost	Throughput costs represent the costs associated with conversion of resources into a finished product and do not represent costs that will change in the event of selecting between different alternative associated with abandoning a segment.
Total quality management	Total quality management strives to please customers by improving their products. **Total quality management (TQM)** represents an organizational commitment to customer-focused performance that emphasizes both quality and continuous improvement.
Transaction Marketing	Transaction marketing involves attracting customers for a single sale.
Transfer pricing	Transfer pricing is the charge made between affiliates for products or services. Transfer prices may be at any level including cost and market and do not relate to the establishment of prices to external customers.
Trojan horse	A Trojan horse (like the wooden horse in Helen of Troy) is a program that appears to have a useful function but that contains a hidden and unintended function that presents a security risk (appears to be legitimate but performs an illicit activity when it is run).
Trough Business cycle	A trough is the lowest level of economic activity. It is the point where real GDP is at its lowest level in the cycle and unemployment is at its highest level in the cycle. The trough of a business cycle is an economic low point with no positive indicators for the future. It is characterized by unused productive capacity and an unwillingness to risk new investment.
Uncontrollable risks	Uncontrollable risks are, by definition, not within the ability of the manager to mitigate. Like sunk costs that will not change regardless of priorities, uncontrollable risk is not useful when prioritizing risk.
Unilateral	Action taken by a single nation acting on its own is referred to as unilateral.
Unipolar	Power concentrated in a single nation is referred to as a unipolar distribution of power.
Universal resource	A URL is a string of characters conforming to a standardized format which refers to

locator (URL)	a resource on the Internet. Data for data mining purposes is seldom, if ever, on the Internet. That would be way too slow.
Unix	The Unix operating system is divided into two pieces: the kernel and the shell. The kernel handles tasks of memory allocation, device input/output, process allocation, security, and user access. The shell handles the user's input and invokes other programs to run commands
Valid code tests	Valid code tests are tests where codes entered are checked against valid values in a master file. Valid code tests are effective with fields when the correct values can be identified in advance and set up in the table.
Value added costs	Value added costs are those resource uses that provide value to the consumer. The cost of inventorying products, generally moving, handling and storing them, does not add value to the product and is generally considered one of the most significant non-value activities/costs that a manufacturer should reduce because it can be controlled.
Value added networks	Value added networks are privately owned communications networks that provide additional services beyond standard data transmission. VANs provide good security because they are private networks.
Value added tax	A value added tax is an incremental tax, not a reduction in tariffs.
Value chain analysis.	Value chain analysis is concerned with the additional value a product gains by passing through all the activities in the production chain. The process of developing macro level flow charts of business processes that produce products or services and then identifying the value added by each process is referred to as value chain analysis.
Variable Costing	Variable costs are those costs that increase or decrease with changes in production. Variable costs do not embrace all costs that will change in the event of different alternatives, only changes in production. Variable (sometimes called direct) costing is used for the benefit of internal users, Variable costs excludes fixed costs from product (inventoried) costs and thereby produces a contribution margin based income statement highly useful to internal managers in computing break even points and other analysis of performance.
Variable overhead efficiency	The formula for the variable overhead efficiency variance is computed as budgeted variable overhead based on standard hours minus budgeted variable overhead based on actual hours. The sole difference between these two calculated amounts is the use of actual compared to standard hours for overhead.
Virtual memory	Virtual memory is memory where portions of a program that are not being executed are stored, but it is not real memory. It is actually a part of disk storage. When the part of the program that is being stored in virtual memory is to be executed, that part of the program is retrieved and stored in real memory.
Virtual private network (VPN)	A virtual private network (VPN) provides an encrypted communication tunnel across the internet that allows remote users to secure access to a network.
Virus	A virus is a piece of computer program that inserts itself into some other

	program. Virus protection software can be utilized to protect against viruses. One of the benefits of such software is definitely of that it can be installed and forgotten. Virus protection software must be continually updated because new viruses are being continually developed.
WAN	WANs allow national and international communications. They usually employ non-dedicated public communications channels (fiber optic, terrestrial microwave, or satellite) as their communications media. WAN communication services may be provided by value added networks or by Internet-based networks. If a WAN is provided by an Internet-based network, it will not be as secure as a VAN.
Web crawler	A web crawler (also known as a web spider or web robot) is a program which browses the web in a methodical, automated manner. Web crawlers are mainly used to create a copy of visited web pages for later processing by a search engine. Web crawlers can also be used for automating maintenance tasks on a web site. Web crawlers can also be used to gather specific types of information from web pages.
Zero balance account	Zero balance account banking represents an account that maintains a zero balance. Zero balance accounts are accompanied by a master or parent account that serves to fund any negative balance and is designed to maximize the availability of idle cash, not control receipts.
Zero-coupon bonds	Zero-coupon bonds has, in effect, a fixed stated rate of return that would require assignment of a premium or discount to the underlying security to produce a market rate of interest if that market yield is different from the stated rate.

MOBILE APP

Dear reader,

Thanks for purchasing   CPA BEC Review notes, I hope this review note has added value to your memory bank to succeed in your forthcoming BEC examination.

As you know time is very essential, in my opinion you should use every minutes of time in a productive way. Keeping in mind the importance of time, I have developed this free mobile APP, which you can refer when you are at not at home.

This mobile app has two sections. Section (1) – short description of various terminologies of BEC section. This will help you understand and memorize terminologies, so that you can apply these concepts when you are writing your BEC examination. Section (2) – multiple choice questions and answers. I tried to solve few questions and answer in very different way.

I promise you; I   will update this mobile app regularly.

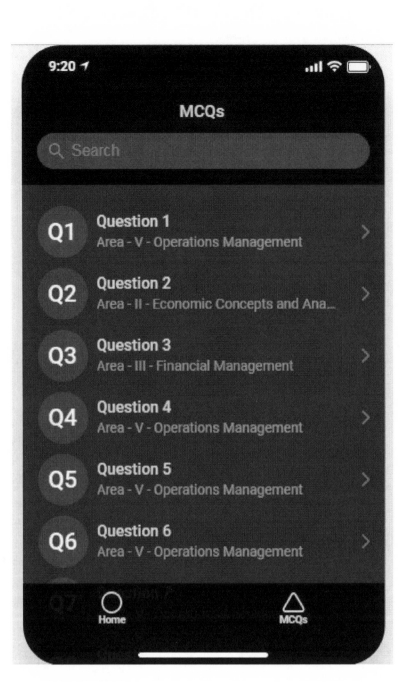

2019 CPA BEC
Area - II - Economic Concepts and
Analysis

Children

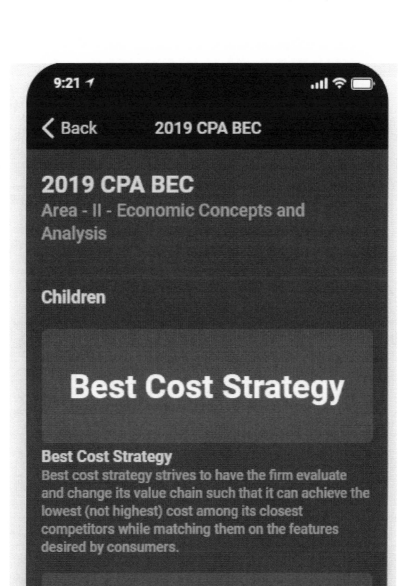

Best Cost Strategy

Best Cost Strategy
Best cost strategy strives to have the firm evaluate
and change its value chain such that it can achieve the
lowest (not highest) cost among its closest
competitors while matching them on the features
desired by consumers.

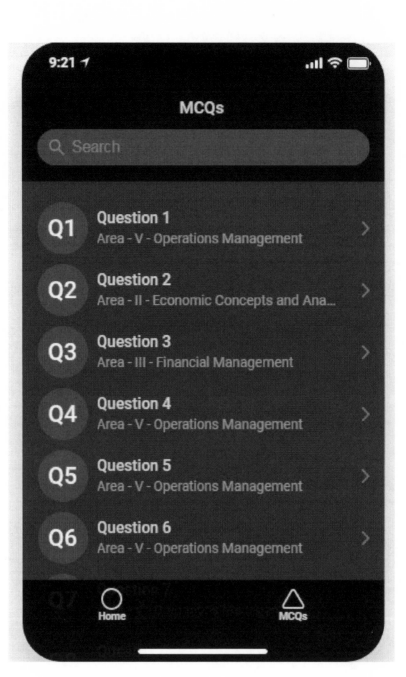

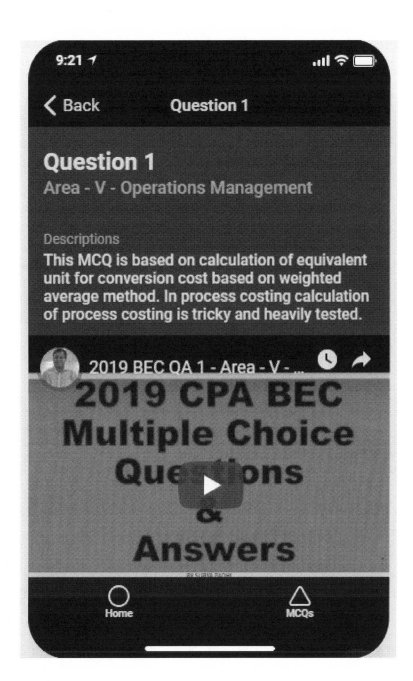

Scan below QR code to get this free mobile APP

SCAN TO OPEN APP

ABOUT THE AUTHOR

Surya Padhi is a chartered accountant and practicing SAP ERP finance consultant

Made in the USA
San Bernardino, CA
17 December 2019